First World War
and Army of Occupation
War Diary
France, Belgium and Germany

29 DIVISION
Headquarters, Branches and Services
General Staff
1 April 1916 - 31 May 1916

WO95/2280/2

The Naval & Military Press Ltd
www.nmarchive.com
Published in association with The National Archives

Published by

The Naval & Military Press Ltd

Unit 10 Ridgewood Industrial Park,

Uckfield, East Sussex,

TN22 5QE England

Tel: +44 (0) 1825 749494

www.naval-military-press.com

www.nmarchive.com

This diary has been reprinted in facsimile from the original. Any imperfections are inevitably reproduced and the quality may fall short of modern type and cartographic standards.

© **Crown Copyright**
Images reproduced by permission of The National Archives, London, England, 2015.

Contents

Document type	Place/Title	Date From	Date To
Heading	General Staff 29th Division April 1916 Appendices attached :)-1 to III & sub files		
Heading	War Diary General Staff 29th Division for the month of April 1916 Volume XIV		
War Diary		01/04/1916	30/04/1916
Miscellaneous	Appx F 1-6.		
Miscellaneous	31 Div./S/13 Appendix I.	29/03/1916	29/03/1916
Operation(al) Order(s)	31 Division Order No. 9	30/03/1916	30/03/1916
Operation(al) Order(s)	31st Division Order No. 10.	31/03/1916	31/03/1916
Miscellaneous	Movement Table Issued With 31st Division Order No. 10		
Miscellaneous	Headquarters, 31st Division.	31/03/1916	31/03/1916
Miscellaneous	C Form (Original). Messages And Signals.	01/04/1916	01/04/1916
Miscellaneous		31/03/1916	31/03/1916
Operation(al) Order(s)	30th Division Order No. 26	01/04/1916	01/04/1916
Operation(al) Order(s)	29th Division Order No. 27	02/04/1916	02/04/1916
Miscellaneous	March Table "D" for April 3rd 1916.	03/04/1916	03/04/1916
Miscellaneous	March Table "E" for April 4th 1916.	04/04/1916	04/04/1916
Miscellaneous	Headquarters, 87th Brigade. Headquarters, 31st Division (for information)	02/04/1916	02/04/1916
Miscellaneous	36th Div. No. G.S/34/797	31/03/1916	31/03/1916
Miscellaneous	Appx II 1-4		
Miscellaneous	Headquarters, 29th Divisional Artillery 4th April 1916. Appendix II	04/04/1916	04/04/1916
Miscellaneous	Appendix A		
Miscellaneous	Appendix B.	05/04/1916	05/04/1916
Miscellaneous	Transcript Of Pencil Handwritten Appendices To Report Of Operations On 6 Apr 16 War Diary Of HQ 26 Division Appendix A	06/04/1916	06/04/1916
Miscellaneous	Report On Operations Which Took Place On Night 6th April 1916.	06/04/1916	06/04/1916
Miscellaneous	A Form. Messages And Signals.		
Miscellaneous	Appx. III 1		
Miscellaneous	Off Or. H. Totals 65. 1562. 770		
Miscellaneous	Previous copies to be destroyed. Position Of Headquarters. VIII Corps. Appendix III.	07/04/1916	07/04/1916
Operation(al) Order(s)	29th Division Order No. 28.	10/04/1916	10/04/1916
Miscellaneous	March Table "F" for April 12th 1916.	12/04/1916	12/04/1916
Miscellaneous	March Table "G" for April 13th 1916.	13/04/1916	13/04/1916
Miscellaneous	Previous copies to be destroyed. Position Of Headquarters. VIII Corps	14/04/1916	14/04/1916
Miscellaneous	29th Division Dispositions At 10-0 P.M. on 14th April, 1916.	14/04/1916	14/04/1916
Miscellaneous	29th Divisional Conference No. 7. held on 16th April, 1916.	16/04/1916	16/04/1916
Miscellaneous	VIII Corps. G.426.	17/04/1916	17/04/1916
Operation(al) Order(s)	29th Division Order No. 29.	17/04/1916	17/04/1916
Miscellaneous	86th Brigade.	18/04/1916	18/04/1916
Miscellaneous	29th Division Dispositions At 10-0 a.m. on April, 29th 1916.	29/04/1916	29/04/1916

Miscellaneous	86th Brigade.	19/04/1916	19/04/1916
Miscellaneous	86th Brigade.	24/04/1916	24/04/1916
Miscellaneous Map	Headquarters, VIIIth Corps.	30/04/1916	30/04/1916
Miscellaneous	Disposition Of 29th Division.	21/04/1916	21/04/1916
Miscellaneous	Amendments to "29th Division Defence Scheme".	21/04/1916	21/04/1916
Miscellaneous	VIII Corps. G. 471. 29th Division.	20/04/1916	20/04/1916
Miscellaneous	Message	25/04/1915	25/04/1915
Miscellaneous			
Miscellaneous		25/04/1916	25/04/1916
Miscellaneous	Programme For Corps Commander-25th April, 1916.	25/04/1916	25/04/1916
Miscellaneous	C Form (Duplicate). Messages And Signals.		
Miscellaneous	A Form. Messages And Signals.		
Miscellaneous	VIII Corps. G.528 29th Division.	25/04/1916	25/04/1916
Miscellaneous	Transcript Of Message To VIII Corps From 29th Div 25 April 16. In reply to G528	25/04/1916	25/04/1916
Miscellaneous	A Form. Messages And Signals.		
Miscellaneous	C Form. (Duplicate). Messages And Signals.		
Heading	General Staff 29th Division May 1916		
Heading	War Diary General Staff 29th Division for the month of May 1916 Volume XV		
War Diary		01/05/1916	31/05/1916
Miscellaneous	29th Division Dispositions At 10-0 P.M. on 5th May. 1916. Appendix 1	05/05/1916	05/05/1916
Miscellaneous	29th Divisional Conference No. 8 Held on 7th May, 1916. Appendix 2	07/05/1916	07/05/1916
Miscellaneous	Agenda For Conference On 7/5/16.	07/05/1916	07/05/1916
Operation(al) Order(s)	29th Division Order No. 31. Appendix 3	06/05/1916	06/05/1916
Miscellaneous	Headquarters, VIII Corps. Appendix 4	09/05/1916	09/05/1916
Miscellaneous	29th Division Training Programme.		
Miscellaneous	G.S. Memorandum No. 29. App. A.	01/02/1916	01/02/1916
Miscellaneous	Courses Of Instruction. App B.		
Miscellaneous	The Strength of the 88th Brigade is as follows		
Miscellaneous	29th Division Dispositions At 10. p.m. On May 10th 1916. Appendix 5	10/05/1916	10/05/1916
Operation(al) Order(s)	31st Division Order No. 18 Appendix 6	14/05/1916	14/05/1916
Miscellaneous	31st Division Order No. 18. March Table.		
Miscellaneous			
Operation(al) Order(s)	29th Division Order No. 32. Appendix 7	16/05/1916	16/05/1916
Miscellaneous	29th Division Dispositions at 10.O a.m. on May 19th 1916. Appendix 8.	19/05/1916	19/05/1916
Miscellaneous	Confidential. VIII Corps. G. 959. Appendix 9	19/05/1916	19/05/1916
Miscellaneous	29th Division. (a) Offensive Preparations.		
Miscellaneous	(b) Defensive Preparations		
Miscellaneous	(c) Training Arrangements.		
Miscellaneous	VIII Corps G. 1030.	23/05/1916	23/05/1916
Miscellaneous	29th Divisional Conference No. 9 Held on 23rd May 1916. Appendix 10	23/05/1916	23/05/1916
Operation(al) Order(s)	31st Division Order No 19. Appendix 11	22/05/1916	22/05/1916
Miscellaneous	Notes For Corps Conference At 10.O am. on 26th May 1916. Appendix 12	26/05/1916	26/05/1916
Operation(al) Order(s)	29th Division Order No. 33. Appendix 13	26/05/1916	26/05/1916
Miscellaneous	87th Bde For Your Information Return pse.	29/05/1916	29/05/1916
Operation(al) Order(s)	36th Division Order No. 27 Appendix 14	28/05/1916	28/05/1916
Miscellaneous	Table Of Reliefs		
Operation(al) Order(s)	36th Division Order No. 28.	29/05/1916	29/05/1916

Miscellaneous	29th Division Daily Summary. for Period 6 a.m. 30/4/16 to 6 a.m. 1/5/16. Appx 15	30/04/1916	30/04/1916
Miscellaneous	29th Division Daily Summary. for Period from 6 a.m. 1/5/16 to 6 a.m. 2/5/16.	01/05/1916	01/05/1916
Miscellaneous	29th Divisional Daily Summary. for Period from 6 a.m. 2/5/16 to 6 a.m. 3/5/16.	02/05/1916	02/05/1916
Miscellaneous	29th Division Daily Summary for Period from 6 a.m. 3/5/16 to 6 a.m. 4/5/16.	03/05/1916	03/05/1916
Miscellaneous	29th Division Daily Summary. for Period from 6 a.m. 4/5/16 to 6 a.m. 5/5/16	04/05/1916	04/05/1916
Miscellaneous	29th Division Daily Summary. for Period from 6 a.m. 5/5/16 to 6 a.m. 6/5/16.	05/05/1916	05/05/1916
Miscellaneous	29th Division Daily Summary. for Period from 6.O a.m. 6/5/16 to 6.O a.m. 7/5/16.	06/05/1916	06/05/1916
Miscellaneous	29th Division Daily Summary for Period from 6 a.m. 7/5/16 to 6 a.m. 8/5/16.	07/05/1916	07/05/1916
Miscellaneous	29th Division Daily Summary. for Period from 6 a.m. 8/5/16 to 6 a.m. 9/5/16.	08/05/1916	08/05/1916
Miscellaneous	29th Division Daily Summary. for Period from 6 a.m. 9/5/16 to 6 a.m. 10/5/16.	09/05/1916	09/05/1916
Miscellaneous	29th Division Daily Summary. For Period From 6 a.m. 10/5/16 to 6 a.m. 11/5/16.	10/05/1916	10/05/1916
Miscellaneous	29th Division Daily Summary. For Period From 6 a.m. 11/5/16 to 6 a.m. 12/5/16.	11/05/1916	11/05/1916
Miscellaneous	29th Division Daily Summary. For Period From 6 a.m. 12/5/16 to 6 a.m. 13/5/16.	12/05/1916	12/05/1916
Miscellaneous	29th Division Daily Summary. For Period From 6 a.m. 13/5/16 to 6 a.m. 14/5/16.	13/05/1916	13/05/1916
Miscellaneous	29th Division Daily Summary. For Period From 6 a.m. 14/5/16 to 6 a.m. 15/5/16	14/05/1916	14/05/1916
Miscellaneous	29th Division Daily Summary. For Period From 6 a.m. 15/5/16 to 6 a.m. 16/5/16.	15/05/1916	15/05/1916
Miscellaneous	29th Division Daily Summary. For Period From 6 a.m. 16/5/16 to 6 a.m. 17/5/16.	16/05/1916	16/05/1916
Miscellaneous	29th Division Daily Summary. For Period From 6 a.m. 17/5/16 to 6 a.m. 18/5/16.	17/05/1916	17/05/1916
Miscellaneous	29th Division Daily Summary. For Period From 6 a.m. 18/5/16 to 6 a.m. 19/5/16.	18/05/1916	18/05/1916
Miscellaneous	29th Division Daily Summary. for Period From 6.O. a.m. on 19/5/16 to 6.O.a.m. on 20/5/16.	19/05/1916	19/05/1916
Miscellaneous	29th Division Daily Summary. For Period From 6 a.m. 20/5/16 to 6 a.m. 21/5/16.	20/05/1916	20/05/1916
Miscellaneous	29th Division Daily Summary. For Period From 6. a.m. 21/5/16 to 6. a.m. 22/5/16.	21/05/1916	21/05/1916
Miscellaneous	29th Division Daily Summary. for Period From 6.a.m. 22/5/16 to 6.a.m. 23/5/16.	22/05/1916	22/05/1916
Miscellaneous	29th Division Daily Summary & For Period From 6. a.m. 23/5/16 to 6. a.m. 24/5/16.	23/05/1916	23/05/1916
Miscellaneous	29th Division Daily Summary. For Period From. 6. a.m. 24/5/16 to 6. a.m. 25/5/16.	24/05/1916	24/05/1916
Miscellaneous	29th Division Daily Summary. For Period From 6. a.m. 25/5/16 to 6. a.m. 26/6/16	25/05/1916	25/05/1916
Miscellaneous	29th Division Daily Summary. Period From 6. a.m. 26/5/16 to 6. a.m. 27/5/16.	26/05/1916	26/05/1916
Miscellaneous	29th Division Daily Summary. For Period From 6. a.m. 27/5/16 to 6. a.m. 28/5/16.	27/05/1916	27/05/1916

Miscellaneous	29th Division Daily Summary. For Period From. 6. a.m. 28/5/16 to 6. a.m. 29/5/16	28/05/1916	28/05/1916
Miscellaneous	29th Divisional Summary. For Period From 6. a.m. 29/5/16 to 6. a.m. 30/5/16	29/05/1916	29/05/1916
Miscellaneous	29th Division Daily Summary for Period From 6. a.m. 30/5/16 to 6. a.m. 31/5/16. Appendix 15	30/05/1916	30/05/1916

GENERAL STAFF

29th DIVISION

APRIL 1916

Appendices attached :) - 1 to III & sub files

Confidential

War Diary

General Staff

29th Division

For the month of

April 1916.

Volume XIV

Army Form C. 2118.

WAR DIARY – GENERAL STAFF 29th Division.

or

INTELLIGENCE SUMMARY.

(*Erase heading not required.*)

1916.

Instructions regarding War Diaries and Intelligence Summaries are contained in F.S. Regs., Part II. and the Staff Manual respectively. Title pages will be prepared in manuscript.

Place	Date	Hour	Summary of Events and Information	Remarks and references to Appendices
	1st April.		29th Divisional Headquarters at BEAUQUESNE. G.O.C., G.S.O.1 and A.A. & Q.M.G. attended a Conference in the morning at VIII Corps Headquarters at MARIEUX. 87th Brigade at AMPLIERS. Divisional Conference at BEAUQUESNE at 5.p.m.	
	2nd April.		87th Brigade (less 1 Battalion) moved to MAILLY-MAILLET, ENGLEBELMER and ACHEUX respectively, Headquarters at MAILLY-MAILLET. Appendix 1 comprises:- 1. 31st Division /S/13 asking for our date for taking over 31st Division line and suggesting certain arrangements. 2. 31st Division Order No.9 dated 30/3/16 and 31st Division Order No.10 with March Table attached. 3. 29th Division C.G.S.36 dated 31/3/16 in reply to 31st Division /S/13 (above) with answering message from 31st Division attached. 4. 29th Division Order No. 26 reference arrangements for taking over the line. 5. 29th Division Order No. 27 dated 2nd April, 1916 with March Tables for 3rd and 4th April attached. 6. 29th Division D.O. No. 27 dated 2nd April instructions to Brigade Machine Gun Companies in accordance with 36th Division G.S./34/797 of 31/3/16 attached.	(App.1(4))

Army Form C. 2118.

WAR DIARY - GENERAL STAFF 29th Division.

INTELLIGENCE SUMMARY

(Erase heading not required.)

Instructions regarding War Diaries and Intelligence Summaries are contained in F.S. Regs., Part II. and the Staff Manual respectively. Title pages will be prepared in manuscript.

Place	Date	Hour	Summary of Events and Information	Remarks and references to Appendices
	1916. 3rd April			
	3rd April.		Three Battalions 87th Brigade took over the front line from junction of Q.17.11 and Q.17.12 to Q.4.b.Central from the 92nd and 93rd Brigades on the night of 3/4th Apl. vide Appendix 1. (4)	(App.1 (4))
			29th Division Headquarters moved to ACHEUX at 11.a.m. from BEAUQUESNE.	
	4th April.		86th Brigade moved to new area ACHEUX (2 Battalions), ENGLEBELMER (1 Battalion), BEAUSSART (1 Battalion). 88th Brigade moved to area LOUVENCOURT (4 Battalions), ARQUEVES and BELLE EGLISE (1 Battalion).	(App.1(5))
			1 Battalion 87th Brigade moved to MAILLY-MAILLET vide March Table E attached to Appendix 1(5).	
			29th Division took over command of front line at 9.a.m.	

T2134. Wt. W708-776. 500000. 4/15. Sir J. C. & S.

Army Form C. 2118.

WAR DIARY - GENERAL STAFF & 29th Division.

or INTELLIGENCE SUMMARY.

(Erase heading not required.)

Instructions regarding War Diaries and Intelligence Summaries are contained in F. S. Regs., Part II. and the Staff Manual respectively. Title pages will be prepared in manuscript.

1916.

Place	Date	Hour	Summary of Events and Information	Remarks and references to Appendices
	5th April.		13th Yorks and Lancs. Regiment remained in our Sector at MAILLY-MAILLET as Mining Battalion and are Corps Troops (vide Appendix 1 (2))	(App.1 (2))
			The G.O.C. inspected the front line held by the 87th Brigade.	
			At 3. a.m. a patrol of 1 Officer (Phillimore) and 1 man, S.W.Bs, went out and did not return. Another patrol from the Border Regt. went out at 9.30. p.m. and returned without an Officer (2nd Lieut Crossland) and 1 man (vide Appendix (2)2)	(App.2 (2))
			29th Divisional Artillery took over Right Sections of Batteries from 31st Divisional Artillery on night 5th/6th. (vide Appendix 2 (1))	(App.2 (1))
North of AUCHONVILLERS.	6th April.		Corps Commander visited G.O.C.. G.O.C. visited position for new Northern Divisional Observation Posts	
			At 9.p.m. enemy raided our trenches about Q.6.3.1. after subjecting the trenches between MESNIL and AUCHONVILLERS and the REDAN to a heavy bombardment between 9.p.m. and 10.30. p.m. vide Appendix 2 (3) total casualties were 1 Officer and 33 Other Ranks killed 8 Officers and 42 Other Ranks wounded, 28 Other Ranks missing, grand total 112. Half our Artillery was engaged in warding off the attack. Remainder of 6½ Batteries in front did not take over till the 7th April.	(App 2 (3))
			29th Divisional Artillery took over Left Sections of Batteries from 31st Divisional Artillery on nights 6/7th. (vide Appendix 2 (1))	(App.2 (1))

T2134. Wt. W708—776. 500000. 4/15. Sir J. C. & S.

Army Form C. 2118.

WAR DIARY - GENERAL STAFF 29th Division.
or
INTELLIGENCE SUMMARY.
(*Erase heading not required.*)

Instructions regarding War Diaries and Intelligence Summaries are contained in F.S. Regs., Part II. and the Staff Manual respectively. Title pages will be prepared in manuscript.

1916.

Place	Date	Hour	Summary of Events and Information	Remarks and references to Appendices
	7th April	10.a.m.	(vide Appendix 2 (1). The C.R.A. 29th Division took over control of Artillery on our front at A Course commenced at the Trench Mortar School VALHEUREUX ; personnel of Stokes T.M.Batteries, 3 Medium T.M.Batteries, 1 Heavy T.M. Battery and 33 extra R.A. personnel as reinforcements attended. Appendix 2.comprises:- 1 Instructions for relief of 31st Division Artillery dated 4th April. 2.Report on 2 patrols sent out by 87th Brigade on night 4th/5th and 5th/6th and on the disappearance of 2 Officers and 2 men. 3.Report on Operations which took place on the night of 6th April 1916 with messages G.A.81 and G.702, previously sent to VIII Corps attached. 4.G.715 reference shelling of a party of Yorks and Lancs.	(App.2 (1)
	8th April.		Royal Inniskilling Fusiliers relieved South Wales Borderers during the night of 7/8th on the right of our line. G.O.C. visited site for new Southern Divisional Observation Post, above HAMEL, and then inspected Redoubt Line.	

Army Form C. 2118.

WAR DIARY GENERAL STAFF 29th Division.
INTELLIGENCE SUMMARY.
(Erase heading not required.)

Instructions regarding War Diaries and Intelligence Summaries are contained in F. S. Regs., Part II. and the Staff Manual respectively. Title pages will be prepared in manuscript.

1916.

Place	Date	Hour	Summary of Events and Information	Remarks and references to Appendices
Worcester Regt.	9th April.		The following Officers attended a Seniors Officer's Course at FLEXECOURT:- Major Wilson R.M.F., Lieut. Colonel Pollard Border Regt, Major Kerans 4th Worcester Regt. The 147th Brigade R.F.A., B and C. Batteries 152nd How. Brigade, 369th and 370th Batteries R.F.A. with all Brigade Ammunition Columns moved from DOMART to AMPLIERS and FRESCHEVILLERS. At about 3.30 p.m. a party of about 200 13th Yorks and Lancs. were shelled while marching on the road between AUCHONVILLERS and MAILLY-MAILLET, vide Appendix 2 (4)	(App. 2 (4))
	10th April.		A Conference was held at Divisional Headquarters at 10 a.m. to decide on the best methods of taking offensive action against BEAUMONT HAMEL. A quiet day.	

Army Form C. 2118.

WAR DIARY – GENERAL STAFF 29th Division.
or
INTELLIGENCE SUMMARY
(Erase heading not required.)

1916.

Instructions regarding War Diaries and Intelligence Summaries are contained in F. S. Regs., Part II. and the Staff Manual respectively. Title pages will be prepared in manuscript.

Place	Date	Hour	Summary of Events and Information	Remarks and references to Appendices
	11th April.		A quiet day, rained heavily.	
	12th April.		Rained all day. The 86th Brigade commenced relieving the 87th Brigade in the front line trenches. One Battalion 86th Brigade relieving the Battalion 87th Brigade in the Centre Sector, 2 Battalions of the 88th Brigade moved up to ENGLEBELMER and MAILLY-MAILLET into Divisional Reserve and 2 Battalions 87th Brigade moved back to ACHEUX and LOUVENCOURT becoming Corps Reserve. Vide 29th Division Operation Order No.28 and attached March Table F. (Appendix 3 (2)). The Corps Commander visited the G.O.C. at 5. p.m. at Divisional H.Q. G.S.O.1 and G.S.O.3 visited the trenches from TIPPERARY Avenue to Q.10.7.	(App.3 (2))

Army Form C. 2118.

WAR DIARY - GENERAL STAFF 29th Division.
or
INTELLIGENCE SUMMARY.
(Erase heading not required.)

Instructions regarding War Diaries and Intelligence Summaries are contained in F.S. Regs., Part II. and the Staff Manual respectively. Title pages will be prepared in manuscript.

1916.

Place	Date	Hour	Summary of Events and Information	Remarks and references to Appendices
	13th April.		The G.O.C., G.S.O.1½, G.S.O.2 all Brigadiers, C.R.A. and Divisional Grenadier Officer went to witness a demonstration of the firing of various types of Trench Mortars also the effect of smoke candles at the Trench Mortar School VALHEUREUX during the afternoon. The following moves took place:- 2 Battalions of the 86th Brigade took over the front line from the 87th Brigade. Headquarters and 1 Battalion 87th Bde moved to LOUVENCOURT, 1 Battalion 87th Brigade moved to ACHEUX. 3 Battalions 88th Brigade moved to ENGLEBELMER, BEAUSSART and MAILLY-MAILLET respectively. 87th Field Ambulance moved to LOUVENCOURT also the Divisional Train. Vide March Table G. attached to 29th Division Operation No 28 (App.3 (2)). Relief of Battalions in the front line was reported complete at 11.p.m. A quiet day, a few shells were dropped in AUCHONVILLERS.	(App.3. (2))
	14th April.		Trench Mortar Course at VALHEUREUX finished. The 2 Medium and 1 Light T.M. Battery lent us by the 31st Division returned to their Division and were replaced by our own Batteries. X 29 and 87/1 and 87/2 Light Batteries proceeded to SAILLY - AU-BOIS for temporary attachment to the 48th Division. A quiet day, some hostile machine gun fire at night (14/15th) on SUNKEN Road on our left. G.S.O.1 and G.S.O.2 visited the trenches in Centre Sector.	

T2134. Wt. W708-776. 500000. 4/15. Sir J. C. & S.

Army Form C. 2118.

WAR DIARY - GENERAL STAFF 29th Division.
or
INTELLIGENCE=SUMMARY.
(Erase heading not required.)

Instructions regarding War Diaries and Intelligence Summaries are contained in F. S. Regs., Part II. and the Staff Manual respectively. Title pages will be prepared in manuscript.

1916.

Place	Date	Hour	Summary of Events and Information	Remarks and references to Appendices
	15th April.		G.O.C. and G.S.O.1 visited the trenches of the 36th Division East of THIEPVAL in the morning. G.S.O.2 visited the trenches in Centre and Left Sectors and inspected work done on TIPPERARY Avenue.	
	16th April.		4 Officers and 3 N.C.Os R.F.A. attended the Junior Artillery School Course at HAVERNAS. Lieut. Ball (Divnl. Grenadier Officer) attended the 1st Course at the Central Light T.M.School at HESDIN. Major MEIKLEJOHN, Border Regt. was appointed to command the 1st Essex Regt. in place of Lieut. Colonel Clutterbuck, wounded. A Divisional Conference was held at Divisional H.Q. at 11.a.m. Notes on this Conference are attached to Appendix 3 (5). G.O.C. visited the trenches in the afternoon also the G.S.O.3. A quiet day.	(App.3 (5))

Army Form C. 2118.

WAR DIARY - GENERAL STAFF 29th Division.
or
INTELLIGENCE SUMMARY.
(Erase heading not required.)

Instructions regarding War Diaries and Intelligence Summaries are contained in F. S. Regs., Part II. and the Staff Manual respectively. Title pages will be prepared in manuscript.

1916.

Place	Date	Hour	Summary of Events and Information	Remarks and references to Appendices
	17th April.		1 Officer and 8 N.C.Os proceeded to CAMIERS to undergo a course in the Lewis Gun.	
			G.S.O.2 visited the Left trenches via FOURTH Avenue. The Corps Commander came to the see the G.O.C. in the evening, he said it had been decided not to move Divisional H.Q. forwards in case of an offensive. There was rather more hostile artillery activity; and we had 3 casualties.	
	18th April.		A demonstration of the German Flammenwerfer and Lacrymatory bombs was given by the Fourth Army Chemical Adviser at ACHEUX at 9.a.m. 50 men from each Battalion attended. Rained all day. G.S.O.1 visited the Left and Centre sectors of the trenches during the morning accompanied by the G.S.O.2 and 3 of the VIII Corps. 2 N.C.O.s from 29th Divisional Squadron went to CAMIERS to attend a Hotchkiss Gun Course.	

Army Form C. 2118.

WAR DIARY - GENERAL STAFF 29th Division.
or
INTELLIGENCE SUMMARY.

(Erase heading not required.)

Instructions regarding War Diaries and Intelligence Summaries are contained in F.S. Regs., Part II. and the Staff Manual respectively. Title pages will be prepared in manuscript.

1916.

Place	Date	Hour	Summary of Events and Information	Remarks and references to Appendices
	19th April		During the night 18/19th a new reserve fire trench was dug by the 88th Brigade from point Q.2.d.8.9. across BROADWAY, TIPPERARY Avenue, CLONMEL Street and CLONMEL Avenue. Wire was also put out along the whole front. G.S.O.2 and Major Armitage G.S.O.2 at G.H.Q. visited the Left Section of trenches via FIFTH Avenue. A Conference was held at Corps Headquarters at 2.15.p.m. the following Officers attended :- G.O.C., G.S.O.1, A.A. & Q.M.G., C.R.A. and C.R.E. (agenda attached to Appendix 3 (6)). Rain all day.	(App.3 (6))
	20th April		G.O.C. visited the right of the line in the morning. G.S.O.1 visited the 36th Division to arrange a scheme of action in the event of the enemy attacking and seizing the AUCHONVILLERS - MESNIL Ridge. 1 Officer and 3 men went to Fourth Army H.Q. to attend a Gas Course.	

T/134. Wt. W708—776. 500000. 4/15. Sir J. C. & S.

Army Form C. 2118.

WAR DIARY - GENERAL STAFF 29th Division.
or
INTELLIGENCE SUMMARY.
(Erase heading not required.)

Instructions regarding War Diaries and Intelligence Summaries are contained in F. S. Regs., Part II. and the Staff Manual respectively. Title pages will be prepared in manuscript.

Place	Date	Hour	Summary of Events and Information	Remarks and references to Appendices
	1916.			
	21st April.	morning.	G.S.O.1 and A.A. & Q.M.G. visited the Centre Sector of trenches in the morning.	
			The Army Commander visited General De Lisle at 3.30 p.m. A quiet day, rained the whole afternoon, trenches very wet and muddy. 2 Officers from the 87th Brigade attended a Trench Mortar Course at	(App. 3.(12))
VALHEUREUX.			Dispositions of Units are shewn in list attached to Appendix 5.(12) There was rather more Artillery fire than usual on both sides. Our Aeroplanes were very active.	
	22nd April.		Rained all day. G.O.C. and G.S.O.2 went to FLIXECOURT to witness a demonstration of the various subjects taught at the School, an Officer from each Battalion, and a Staff Officer from each Brigade also attended. G.S.O.3 visited the Machine Gun positions of 86th Brigade. Brigadier General Stockdale (C.R.A.) left the Division, and was succeeded by Brigadier General Peake, C.M.G. who arrived on the 23rd April.	

Army Form C. 2118.

WAR DIARY – GENERAL STAFF 29th Division.

or

INTELLIGENCE SUMMARY

(Erase heading not required.)

1916.

Instructions regarding War Diaries and Intelligence Summaries are contained in F. S. Regs., Part II. and the Staff Manual respectively. Title pages will be prepared in manuscript.

Place	Date	Hour	Summary of Events and Information	Remarks and references to Appendices
	23rd April.		G.S.O.2 visited the trenches of the Right Sector, they were in a bad state owing to the late heavy rains. The 2nd Course at Fourth Army Infantry School FLIXECOURT commenced. 13 Officers and 13 N.C.Os from the 29th Division attended. Our Artillery shelled the enemy trenches and wire more than usual. Work on bomb proof dug-outs and improvement of communication trenches was continued, also the burrying of Signal wires, etc. A mine was commenced at Q.17.a.43.	
	24th April.		The G.O.C. visited the trenches of the Left Sector. G.S.O.1 and G.S.O.3 visited the Right Observation Post and the trenches of the Right Sector. The 16th Middlesex Regt joined the Division in place of 1st Royal Munster Fusiliers. They were billeted at MAILLY-MAILLET. the 1/5th Royal Scots proceeded to DOULLENS, having been ordered to leave the Division.	

Army Form C. 2118.

WAR DIARY— GENERAL STAFF 29th Division.
or
INTELLIGENCE=SUMMARY.
(Erase heading not required.)

Instructions regarding War Diaries and Intelligence Summaries are contained in F. S. Regs., Part II. and the Staff Manual respectively. Title pages will be prepared in manuscript.

1916.

Place	Date	Hour	Summary of Events and Information	Remarks and references to Appendices
	25th April.		G.S.O.2 and G.S.O.3 visited the Centre and Left Sector of trenches with a view to selecting positions for the various Brigade dumps in the event of a forward move. Captain Mellor, K.R.R.C. took over duties of A.P.M. from Capt. Rigg. The Corps Commander inspected those men in the Division who had been present at the Landing under him in GALLIPOLI, the 25th April being the anniversary of the original landing.	
	26th April.		G.S.O.3 and inspected the Camp returning in the evening. The G.S.O.1 visited the Left Sector of Trenches. The Middlesex Regt. Took over a portion of trenches in the Left Sector during the night 25/26th April. G.S.O.1 visited Centre Sector. The G.O.C. motored to the 29th Division Base at ROUEN accompanied by the ~~Brigadier General H. de B. de L.~~ took over duties as Commanding Divisional Artillery from Brig. General Stockdale.	

Army Form C. 2118.

WAR DIARY GENERAL STAFF 29th Division.
or
INTELLIGENCE SUMMARY.
(Erase heading not required.)

Instructions regarding War Diaries and Intelligence Summaries are contained in F.S. Regs., Part II. and the Staff Manual respectively. Title pages will be prepared in manuscript.

1916.

Place	Date	Hour	Summary of Events and Information	Remarks and references to Appendices
	27th April.		An Order was issued for a Divisional School of Instruction to be formed; Major Ellis 1st Border Regt. was appointed Commandant. Major Campbell lectured to Officers and N.C.Os of the Reserve Brigade (87th Brigade.) in bayonet fighting. A reserve bomb store at FORCEVILLE blew up in the morning.	
	28th April.		The G.O.C. visited the trenches of the Left Sector and examined the work lately done. G.S.O.2 visited the 2 Observation Posts being constructed North and South of our line. The G.S.O.3 visited the trenches on the Left. The trenches are dry and greatly improved since the improvement in the weather.	

Army Form C. 2118.

WAR DIARY - GENERAL STAFF 29th Division.

or

INTELLIGENCE SUMMARY.

(Erase heading not required.)

Instructions regarding War Diaries and Intelligence Summaries are contained in F.S. Regs., Part II. and the Staff Manual respectively. Title pages will be prepared in manuscript.

1916.

Place	Date	Hour	Summary of Events and Information	Remarks and references to Appendices
	29th April.		Artillery has been active on both sides, otherwise a quiet day. Fine. A lecture was given at Divisional H.Q. to certain Officers and N.C.Os on German Military terms. The Corps Commander visited the G.O.C. at Divisional H.Q. at 11.a.m. Final preparations were made for the 2 raids to-night. 1 raid to be made by the South Wales Bdrs (87th Brigade.) at point Q.10.b.8.9., the other by the Hants. Regt. (88th Brigade.) at point Q.17.b.15.20. A Class in bayonet fighting commenced under Major Ellis at the Divisional School.	
	30th April.		29/30th April, one by the 88th Brigade (2nd Hants. Regt.) at point Q.17.b.2.3. due East of MARY REDAN, the other by the 87th Brigade (2nd S.W.Bs) at point Q.10.b.8.9. In the former the enemy's wire was successfully penetrated by means of Bangalore torpedoes but strong opposition was then met with and machine guns opened fire, the enterprise had therefore to be given up. Casualties 1 man killed 2 men wounded. In the latter case the wire cutting party succeeded in penetrating the enemy's wire, but so many casualties had occurred by this time that it was impossible to proceed with the raid. Casualties 7 killed 17 wounded. A detailed report of these raids is attached to Appendix.3 In retaliation to our heavy bombardment the enemy's artillery heavily bombarded front and support trenches on our left, causing 68 casualties of which 10 were killed. During the morning G.S.O.1 visited the Left Sector and G.S.O.2 the Right Sector of Trenches. The G.O.C. visited the Corps Commander at 11.a.m. at Corps Headquarters. Appendix 3 comprises:-	(App. 3 (a))

T2134. Wt. W708—776. 500000. 4/15. Sir J.C. & S.

Army Form C. 2118.

WAR DIARY - GENERAL STAFF 29th Division.
or
INTELLIGENCE SUMMARY.
(Erase heading not required.)

Instructions regarding War Diaries and Intelligence Summaries are contained in F. S. Regs., Part II. and the Staff Manual respectively. Title pages will be prepared in manuscript.

1916.

Place	Date	Hour	Summary of Events and Information	Remarks and references to Appendices
	30th April.		Appendix 3 comprises:- 1. VIII Corps G.282 (Secret) giving positions of H.Q. on 7th April. 2. 29th Division Order No. 28 Reference Brigade Reliefs with March Tables attached. 3. VIII Corps G.384 giving position of H.Q. on 14th April. 4. 29th Division Dispositions on 14th April. 5. Notes on Divisional Conference held on 16 April 1916. 6. VIII Corps G.426 reference Corps Conference to be held on April 19th giving Agenda. 7. 29th Division Order No. 29 dated 17th April, reference division of front line into 2 Sectors. 8. Amended allotment of work dated April 18th. 9. 29th Division Dispositions on April 29th. 10. Report on our 2 raids attempted on 29/30th night. 11. The trench map showing M.G. positions and mines is attached. 12. 29th Division Dispositions on 21st April attached. Appendix 4 comprises:- Daily and Weekly Summaries.	

C. Fuller
Lt.Col.
for G.O.C.
29. Division.

Appx I

1 - 6

Secret

31 Div./ S/13

Appendix I

29th Division.

  Can you inform me the approximate date on which you will be able to commence taking over from this Division your allotted portion of the line, and the number of the brigade with which you propose to effect the relief.

  The brigades of this Division at present holding the front which you are to occupy (Q.17.c.73 to Q.4.Central) are the 92nd Inf.Bde. from Q.17.c.73 to Q.10.b.15 and 93rd Inf.Bde. the remainder of the line.

  The following procedure is suggested for taking over :

  <u>1st Day</u>. 2 front line battalions take over the reserve billets at ENGLEBELMER and ACHEUX of the brigade in front line, the relieved battalions moving out of 29th Division Area.

  <u>2nd Day</u>. The two battalions of the 29th Division from reserve billets take over front line trenches. The relieved battalions march back to reserve billets and become reserve to battalions of 29th Division in front line trenches.

  <u>3rd Day</u>. Reserve battalions 31st Division to be relieved by remainder of the Brigade, 29th Division, taking over and thereupon move out of 29th Division Area.

  It is further suggested that the 2nd April would be a convenient date to commence so as to leave a margin for the relief being completed by the night of the 5th/6th April, if you concur.

        H.W. Stenhouse Major
         for Major-General
D.H.Q.   Commanding 31st Division.
29.3.16.

Reference:
1/10,000
Trench Map.

Copy No. 17

31 DIVISION ORDER No.9

30.3.16.

1. On 2nd April, 29th Division will commence taking over that part of the line at present held by the 31st Division from Q.17.c.73 to Q.4.b Central.

2. On that date the 92nd Inf.Bde. will commence to hand over their front to 87th Bde. of the 29th Division and on completion of the relief will march to BERTRANCOURT.

3. The 93rd Inf.Bde. on same date will commence to hand over that portion of the line held by them from their right at HAWTHORN RIDGE to Q.4.b Central to the 87th Inf.Bde. 29th Division. The remainder of their front from Q.4 b Central to K.34.b.91 will be handed over to the 94th Inf.Bde. commencing on the same date. On relief the 93 Inf.Bde. will march to billets in BUS.

4. The 94th Inf.Bde. will commence to take over that portion of the line between Q.4.b Central and the N edge of LUKE COPSE from the 93rd Inf.Bde. and the 48th Division respectively on the 2nd April.

5. The Artillery relief is to be carried out under instructions to be issued by B.G.,R.A. in consultation with the B.Gs. R.A., of the 29th and 48th Divisions, and under orders issued by G.O.C. R.A., 8th Corps.

6. R.E. and R.A.M.C. adjustments to meet the new portion of the front taken over will be arranged by the C.R.E., and A.D.M.S respectively.

7. These reliefs, with the exception of the R.A. will be completed by the night of the 5th/6th April.

(P.T.O.)

Lieut-Colonel
General Staff
31st Division.

Issued to Signals at

Copy No.1	92 I.B.
No.2	93 I.B.
No.3	94 I.B.
No.4	G.O.C. R.A.,
No.5	C.R.E.
No.6	31 Div. Signals
No.7	31 Div. Train
No.8	A.A.&.Q.M.G.
No.9	" A "
No.10	A.P.M.
No.11	D.A.D.O.S.
No.12	A.D.M.S.
No.13	A.D.V.S.
No.14	Office Copy.
No.15	War Diary.
No.16	**48 Divn.(For information)**
No.17	**29 Divn.(For information)**
No.18	**8th Corps (For information)**

Reference:
1/40,000 Map.
1/10,000 Trench Map.

Copy No. 17

31st DIVISION ORDER NO.10.

31.3.16.

1. With reference to 31st Division Order No.9 of 30th inst. moves will take place in accordance with the attached Movement Table.

    Details of reliefs will be arranged between the Infantry Brigade Commanders concerned.

2. 13 York & Lanc.R. will remain for the present in MAILLY-MAILLET and will not move with the 94th Inf. Bde.

                                                Lieut-Colonel
                                                General Staff
                                                31st Division.

Issued to Signals at.

Copy No.1	92 Inf.Bde.
No.2	93 Inf.Bde.
No.3	94 Inf.Bde.
No.4	G.O.C., R.A.
No.5	C.R.E.
No.6	31 Divl.Signals
No.7	31 Divl.Train
No.8	A.A.& Q.M.G.
No.9	" A "
No.10	A. P. M.
No.11	D.A.D.O.S.
No.12	A.D.M.S.
No.13	A.D.V.S.
No.14	Office Copy
No.15	War Diary
No.16	48th Divn.(For information)
No.17	29th Divn.(For information)
No.18	8th Corps (For information)

Please acknowledge.

ackd

MOVEMENT TABLE ISSUED WITH 31st DIVISION ORDER NO.10   1.

DATE.	UNIT.	FROM.	TO.	REMARKS.
April 2nd.	1 Bn.92 Inf.Bde.	ENGLEBELMER	} BERTRANCOURT	} On relief by 2 Bns.87th Inf. Bde. which will then form Reserve to 92 Inf.Bde.
	1 Bn.92 Inf.Bde.	ACHEUX.	}	
	1 Bn.94 Inf.Bde.	BERTRANCOURT	COLINCAMPS	} Relieving 2 Bns.144 Inf.Bde. which on relief will move out of 31 Divn.Area. On Arrival 2 Bns. 94 Inf.Bde. will come under command of G.O.C 144 Inf.Bde.
	1 Bn.94 Inf.Bde.	BERTRANCOURT	COURCELLES	}
April 3rd.	1 Bn.93 Inf.Bde.	Trenches	ENGLEBELMER	} On relief by Battalions 87th Inf.Bde. 29th Divn.
	1 Bn.93 Inf.Bde.	Trenches	ACHEUX	}
	1 Bn.93 Inf.Bde.	MAILLY-MAILLET	BUS.	}
	1 Bn.93 Inf.Bde.	BEAUSSART		}
	1 Bn.93 Inf.Bde.	Trenches	MAILLY-MAILLET	} On relief by Bn.87th Inf.Bde. 29th Divn. and Bn.94th Inf.Bde.
	1 Bn.93 Inf.Bde.	Trenches	BEAUSSART	}
	1 Bn. 94 Inf.Bde.	COLINCAMPS	Trenches	} Relieving 2 Bns.144 Inf.Bde. one of which will move to COLINCAMPS and the other out of 31st Divn.Area, and also relieving 1 Bn.93 Inf.Bde.
	1 Bn. 94 Inf.Bde.	COURCELLES	Trenches	}
	1 Bn.94 Inf.Bde.	BERTRANCOURT	COURCELLES	On arrival will become reserve to Bns.94 Inf.Bde.in Trenches.

DATE.	UNIT.	FROM.	TO.	REMARKS.
April 4th.	2 Bns. 92 Inf. Bde.	ENGLEBELMER and ACHEUX.	BERTRANCOURT	On relief by 2 Bns. 87th Inf. Bde. 29th Divn. G.O.C. 87th Inf. Bde. assumes command of 87th Inf. Bde. sector of front.
	2 Bns. 93 Inf. Bde.	MAILLY-MAILLET BEAUSSART	BUS	
	1 Bn. 94 Inf. Bde.	COURCELLES	COLINCAMPS	Relieving Bde. of 144th Inf. Bde. which will then move out of 31st Divn. Area.
	1 Bn. 92 Inf. Bde.	BERTRANCOURT	COURCELLES	On arrival will become Reserve to 94 Inf. Bde. G.O.C. 94 Inf. Bde. will assume command of 94 Inf. Bde. sector of front.

SECRET.

HEADQUARTERS,
29th DIVISION.
No. C.G.S 369
Date 31/3/16

Headquarters,
    31st Division.

    In reply to your Secret 31st Division/S/13, of the 29th inst. and with reference to our interview this morning, the following procedure for taking over the front line has been concurred in by your 92nd and 93rd Brigades.

1st Day. On the 2nd April, two Battalions of the 87th Brigade will take over the reserve billets of two Battalions of the 92nd Brigade in ACHEUX and ENGELBELMER, and one Battalion of the 87th Brigade the reserve billets of one Battalion of the 93rd Brigade in MAILLY - MAILLET, the relieved Battalions of the 92nd and 93rd Brigades moving out of the 29th Division Area.

    Advanced parties of about 12 Officers and men from each of the three Battalions of the 87th Brigade will be sent up early to 92and 93rd Brigade Headquarters on the morning of the 2nd April, and will move into the trenches on that afternoon.

2nd Day. On the evening of the 3rd April, the three Battalions of the 87th Brigade in reserve billets will take over the front line, the relieved Battalions of the 92nd and 93rd Brigades marching back to reserve billets, and acting as reserve to Battalions of 87th Brigade in front line trenches.   29th Division Headquarters will move on this day to ACHEUX, and the 87th Brigade Headquarters move to MAILLY - MAILLET. on the 2nd April

3rd Day. On the 4th April, reserve Battalions of the 92nd and 93rd Brigades move out of the 29th Division Area. The

"C" Form (Original).   Army Form C. 2123.
MESSAGES AND SIGNALS.   No. of Message.

Prefix...... Code...... Words...... | Received...... | Sent, or sent out | Office Stamp.
£ s. d. | From...... | At......m
Charges to collect | By...... | To......
Service Instructions. | | By......

Handed in at...... Office ......m. Received ......m.

TO   29th Division

*Sender's Number	Day of Month	In reply to Number	AAA
G 161	1/4/16	G 44	

Your GS 36 now received
and arrangements regarding
transfer are concurred in.

FROM PLACE & TIME   31st Divn   2.30 pm

*This line should be erased if not required.

87th Brigade will come under the orders of the 31st Division on moving into the Area occupied by the Division, and will remain under their orders until 9.0 am. on the 4th April, when the command of the front line will devolve upon the G.O.C. 29th Division.

      Please inform me by wire, whether you concur in these proposals.

[signature]

Lieut. Colonel, G.S.
for Major General
Commanding 29th Division.

31st March 1916.

SECRET.   COPY NO. 3

29th Division Order No. 26

Reference.
Map 57D 1/40,000   1st April 1916.
and 4th Army
Administrative
Map.

1.   On 2nd April, 29th Division will commence taking
over the front line from Junction of Q.17/11 and Q.17/12
by Buckingham Palace Road (exclusive) to Q.4.B. Central,
from the 31st Division.

2.   The 87th Brigade (less 1 Battalion) will march
on the 2nd April via ACHEUX and take over billets from
the 31st Division as follows :-

87th Brigade Headquarters to MAILLY - MAILLET.
1 Battalion in ENGLEBELMER from 92nd Infantry Brigade.
1 Battalion in ACHEUX
1 Battalion in MAILLY - MAILLET from 93rd Infy. Bde.

3.   Advanced parties from the 87th Brigade will be
conveyed to the Headquarters of the 92nd and 93rd
Brigades on the 2nd inst. by motor vehicles, in order to
be shown over the trenches.

4.   The 87th Brigade will relieve the 92nd and 93rd
Infantry Brigades in the trenches on the night 3rd/4th
April.

5.   The remainder of the 87th Brigade will march to
MAILLY - MAILLET via ACHEUX on the 4th April.

6.   The 1st West Riding Field Co. will march to
MAILLY - MAILLET via ACHEUX on the 2nd April, under
orders to be issued by the 87th Brigade.

7.   The 87th Brigade (less 1 Battalion) will come
under the orders of the 31st Division on the 2nd
April on moving into the Area occupied by the 31st
Division, and will remain under their orders until
9.0 am. on the 4th April, when the 29th Division will
take over the command of the front line.

(2).

8. The artillery relief will be carried out under instructions to be issued by G.O.C, R.A. VIIIth Corps. It will be commenced after completion of the infantry relief.

9. Orders for the march of the remainder of the Division will be issued later. All reliefs, except Artillery relief will be completed by night of April 5th/6th, by which date the 29th Division will be concentrated in the billeting area detailed below :-

Eastern Boundary	-	Junction of Q 17/11 and Q 17/12 to Q.4.B. Central.
Southern Boundary	-	Present Xth Corps Boundary, in 4th Army Administrative Map.
Western Boundary	-	As in 4th Army Administrative Map.
Northern Boundary	-	Q.4.B. Central - Q.3a. 7 - 7 - Q. 2. B.46 - and then due West but including LOUVENCOURT.

10. Refilling point for 87th Brigade on 3rd April along ACHEUX - LEAIVILLERS Road at 10.0 am.

11. Divisional Headquarters will move to ACHEUX at 11.0 am. on the 3rd April.

C. G. Fuller

Lieut. Colonel, GVS.
29th Division.

Issued at 5 p.m.

Copy Nos. 1 — 3. General Staff.
        4   86th Brigade.
        5   87th   "
        6   88th   "
     7-11   Headquarters R.A.
      12   Headquarters R.E.
      13   O.C. Divisional Yeomanry.
      14   Off. i/c Signals.
      15   O.C. Divisional Cyclists.
      16   A.A. & Q.M.G.
      17   A.P.M.
18 O.C. Divisional Train   19 A.D.M.S.
20 A.D.V.S.   21 D.A.D.O.S.
22 31st Division   23 36th Division H.Q.
    (for information)   (for information)

SECRET   Copy No. 3 (5)

29TH DIVISION ORDER NO. 27

Ref. 4th Army   2nd April 1916.
Administrative Map.

1. The following units will move on April 3rd and 4th to new billots in accordance with attached march table "D" and "E".

On April 3rd.   Divisional Headquarters.
                R.E. Headquarters.
                18th Mobile Veterinary Section.

On April 4th.   Divisional Yeomanry.
                86th Brigade.
                87th Brigade. (1 Battalion only.)
                88th Brigade.
                London Field Company R.E.
                Kent Field Company R.E.
        87th & 88th Field Ambulances.
                89th Field Ambulance.
                Divisional Train (No. 2 and 4 Coys.)

2. Brigades will notify to these Headquarters the times the head of their columns will be passing the vicinity of 8th Corps Headquarters at MARIEUX.

3. Re-filling point on 4th April for troops moving on 3rd April (vide Table D.) on ACHEUX & LEAIVILLERS ROAD

   Re-filling Point on 5th April for troops moving on 4th April (vide Table E) on ACHEUX - LEAIVILLERS ROAD.

                                        C.G. Fuller.
Issued at... 4 p.m. ....   Lieut. Colonel, G.S.,
                                           29th Division.

Copy Nos. 1-3   General Staff.   19 A.D.M.S.
           4   86th Brigade.   20 A.D.V.S.
           5   87th Brigade.   21 D.A.D.O.S.
           6   88th Brigade.   22 31st Divn. (for information)
         7-11   Headquarters R.A.   23 36th Divn.   "   "
          12   Headquarters R.E.
          13   O.C. Divisional Yeomanry.
          14   Officer i/c Signals.
          15   Camp Commandant.
          16   A.A. & Q.M.G.
          17   A.P.M.
          18   O.C. Divisional Train.

MARCH TABLE "D" for April 3rd 1916.

Unit	From	To	Via.	Remarks.
Divisional Headquartres	BEAUQUESNE	ACHEUX		To arrive ACHEUX after 11. a.m.
R.E. Headquarters	"	"		" " " " "
18th Mobile Veterinary Sect.	"	"		" " " " "

C.G. Fuller
Lieut. Colonel G.S.,
29th Division.

MARCH TABLE "E" for April 4th 1916.

Unit	From	To	via	Remarks
86th Brigade Headquarters	BEAUVAL	ACHEUX		Temporary group under Inf. Brigadier R.E. and Fd Ambce cease to be under command of Brigadier on arrival at Destination. Tail of Column will be clear of BEAUQUESNE by 4 p.m. and of line LOUVENCOURT-LEALVILLERS by 3. p.m.
3 Battalions 86th Bde.	"	ACHEUX (2 Bns.)		
1 Battalion 86th Bde.	CANDAS	ENGLEBELMER (1 Btn.)		
		BEAUSSART (1 Btn.)		
Kent Field Coy.		ENGLEBELMER		
89th Fd. Ambce.		ACHEUX.		
88th Bde. Headquarters	FIENVILLERS	LOUVENCOURT		Temporary group under Inf. Brigadier.Fd Ambce. ceases to be under command of Brigadier on arrival at destination. Head of column will not arrive at BEAUQUESNE before 2. p.m.
1 Battalion	"	LOUVENCOURT (4 Bns.)		
4 Battalions	MONTRELET	ARQUEVES and	FMS DU ROSEL	
	FIEFFES and	BELLE EGLISE (1 Btn.)		
	BONNEVILLE			
88th Fd. Ambce	MONTRELET	ARQUEVES.		
London Fd. Coy R.E.	LONGUEVILLETTE	ACHEUX		Follows 88th Brigade.
87th Brigade (1 Btn.)	AMPLIER	MAILLY - MAILLET	BERTRANCOURT	To be clear of LOUVENCOURT by 3. p.m.
No. 2 Coy. A.S.C.	BEAUVAL	VAUCHELLES	ORVILLE	
No. 4 Coy. A.S.C.	FIEFFES		FIENVILLERS and	
			ORVILLE	
Divisional Yeomanry	HEM	AMPLIER		

MARCH TABLE E. for April 4th 1916 (contd.)

Unit	From	To	Via	Remarks.
87th Field Ambulance	ANPLIER	BEUSSART	BERTRANCOURT	To be clear of LOUVENCOURT BY 3. p.m.

Lieut. Colonel, G.S.,
29th Division.

HEADQUARTERS,
20th DIVISION.

No. DO.17
Date 3/4/16

Headquarters, 87th Brigade.
" ~~51st Division~~ (for information)
" 36th " "

The Machine Gun Companies of the 36th Division
(½ 108th Brigade Machine Gun Company with the 92nd
Brigade, and ½ 107th Brigade Machine Gun Company with
93rd Brigade) will be relieved by the 29th Division
on the 5th April.

Please arrange to relieve the above Machine Gun
Companies on the date mentioned on the front, which
you are taking over.

Acknowledge receipt.

Lieut. Colonel, G.S.
2nd April 1916.   29th Division.

36th Div. No. G.S/34/797

~~31st Division~~
~~29th Division.~~
~~"Q" Branch.~~   )
~~107th Brigade.~~   ) ~~(For information)~~
~~108th Brigade.~~   )

The VIIIth Corps in their G. 157 dated 28. 3. 16. have given instructions that the Machine Gun Companies of the 36th Division (½ 108th Brigade Machine Gun Company with the 92nd Brigade, ½ 107th Brigade Machine Gun Company with the 93rd Brigade) will be relieved by the 29th Division on the 5th April.

Will you be good enough to issue instructions for the relief of the ½ Company in the front which you are taking over.

These Companies when relieved will proceed:-

108th ½ Company to VARENNES.

107th ½ Company to PUCHEVILLERS, which is a distance of about 10 miles from MAILLY, so I shall be glad if the relief can be carried out early in the afternoon, if convenient

H.Q. 36th DIV.
31. 3. 16.

Alick Russell, Lt-Col.
for
MAJOR GENERAL
COMMANDING 36th DIVISION

Appx II

1 — 4

SECRET.

Headquarters, 29th Divisional Artillery,
4th April 1918.   Appendix II
****

Instructions for relief of 31st Divisional Artillery
by 29th Divisional Artillery.

Reference Trench Map BEAUMONT 1/10000 and 1/20000 France 57D.NE2
& Amiens Sheet 1/80000

1. Matters of detail as to carrying out the reliefs will be arranged between group commanders of the Divisional Artilleries concerned in their own groups.
The two group commanders of the 29th Divisional Artillery are the O.C., 17th Brigade R.F.A. at ENGLEBELMER and the O.C. 15th Brigade R.H.A. at MAILLY-MAILLET.

2. Reliefs of H.Q. & Right Sections of batteries concerned will be carried out on the night April 5th/6th and of the Left Sections on the night of April 6th/7th.
The battery commanders of the 29th D.A. will take over control at 9 a.m. 7th April by which time all the personnel will have been exchanged gradually and all arrangements have been entirely completed.

Group commanders will inform D.A.H.Q. by wire at 9.30 a.m. 7th April that control has been taken over and everything is correct.

3. Positions to be taken over have been pointed out to the Brigade & battery commanders concerned - as under :-

		True bearings Normal zone	True bearings Max zone	wagon line (No horses)
'B' R.H.A. (1 Section)	Q.26.a.70.10	30 - 60	9 - 76	(20 Men) MARTINSART ORVILLE Remainder
'L' R.H.A.	Q.13.c.70.60	70 - 85	65 - 93	BERTRANCOURT Gt & MAILLY Wood
'Y' R.H.A.	Q.7.b.35.45	78 - 85	72 - 99	ENG. WOOD P.24.a.3.4
26th 'B' RFA	Q.26.b.10.50	50 - 60	26 - 83	ACHEUX WOOD P.14.c.5.5
92nd "	Q.20.c.35.85	57 - 70	43 - 79	ACHEUX WOOD P.13.a.5.9
13th "	Q.19.b.35.60	58 - 63	47 - 77	
A/132 "	Q.2.c.50.50	95 - 120	73 - 140	BEAUSSART

4. The S.A.A. Section of the 17th Brigade A.C. will relieve the S.A.A. Section of the 31st D.A. at ACHEUX WOOD on 5th April at 7 p.m. and the B.A.C. commander will by that hour have made himself thoroughly acquainted with the exact procedure of supplying ammunition to the Infantry Brigade concerned and their exact location.

5. The exchange of wagon lines will take place at 8 p.m. April 6th/7th.

6. Guns of 31st D.A. will be taken over in position complete with history sheets but less dial sights and guns of 29th D.A. as above will be handed over to the wagon lines.

7. Units will march on April 5th as below under command of the senior officer present -
H.Q. 15th Brigade R.H.A.
H.Q. & Right Section 'B' ---"---
"   "   "   " 'L' ---"---
"   "   "   " 'Y'   ---"---
H.Q. 17th Brigade R.F.A.
H.Q. & Right Section 26th Battery R.F.A.
"   "   "   "   92nd   "   "
"   "   "   "   13th   "   "
S.A.A. Section 17th Brigade R.F.A.

Head of the Column to pass the DOMART bridge E. of DOMART-en-PONTHIEU at 12 noon and proceed along the route BERNEUIL-MONTRELET-BONNEVILLE-BEAUQUESNE-ARQUEVES-ACHEUX.

Head of the column to arrive ACHEUX cross roads at 7 p.m.

The 31st Divisional Artillery will send guides to meet batteries at the cross roads ACHEUX at 7 p.m. to accompany batteries to their wagon lines and also guides from the battery positions to the wagon lines to accompany the personnel to the gun lines.

The Left Sections of the above units (less B RHA) will march at 12 noon April 5th and follow the above instructions on April 6th.

CH Clarke

Major R.A.,

4th April 1916.   Brigade Major 29th Divl.Arty.

Appendix A

Report on Circumstances under which Lieut G. W. Phillimore 3rd K.O.Y.L.I. and No 3/10789 Pte DAVIES 2nd South Wales Borderers, have been reported as missing.

At 0300 (3.0 am) on 5-4-16 Lt Phillimore and Pte Davies went out on patrol to examine ground in front of MARY REDAN. They went out by a sap to the left of the tip of the salient — alone.

At 03.45 (3.45 am) a sentry posted to the right or SOUTH of the tip of the salient saw them — going South.

At about 0400 (4.0 am), as it was beginning to get light, rifle and M.G. fire was heard from the German trenches opposite the salient. Some witnesses say that bombs also were heard. Lieut Phillimore and Pte Davies did not return. The search party mentioned in the Intelligence report found a glove on the wire on the Left of the salient. On the right of the salient, where the patrol probably had been, a search was made towards the German trenches, but without result.

S.L.

Appendix B.

Report on the disappearance of 2/Lieut Crosland and Pte Harvey of the 1/Border Regt. while on Patrol on night of 5-6.4.16.

The patrol was sent out at 21.30 [9.30 pm] by order of Capt Ewbank to patrol for an hour. They left the trenches at about Q.10.4. under instructions to return in an hour.

The L/Cpl's (O'Leary) account is that the patrol advanced for about 150ˣ & about 23.45 [11.45 pm] after seeing the German patrol return moved to the left in search of a shell crater. 2/Lt Crosland left the party when they found themselves obstructed by wire but failed to locate the pit & the patrol turned Right again. They were searching for the way back when a flare went up. This flare was mistaken for a guiding light and the patrol moved towards it. It was then challenged first in English (with a German accent) and then in German. As the patrol was creeping away a second flare went up followed by fire. 2/Lt Crosland was then seen for the last time "standing against the wire". The survivors worked back by rushes to a crater where they lay till enough light enabled them to see where they were and regain their trench. Pte Harvey was then found to be missing and it is thought he was wounded.

AL.

TRANSCRIPT OF PENCIL HANDWRITTEN APPENDICES TO REPORT OF OPERATIONS ON 6 APR 16

WAR DIARY OF HQ 26 DIVISION

APPENDIX A

Report on the circumstances under which Lieut GW Phillimore, 3rd HLI and No 3/10789 Pte Davies, 2nd South Wales Borderers have been reported missing.

At 3.00 am on 5-4-16 Lt Phillimore and Pte Davies went out on patrol to examine ground in front of Mary Redan.

They went out by a sap to the left of the tip of the salient - alone.

At about 03.45 am a sentry posted to the right or South of the tip of the salient saw them going South.

At about 4.00 am, as it was beginning to get light, rifle and MG fire was heard from the German Trenches opposite the salient. Some witnesses say that bombs also were heard. Lieut Phillimore and Pte Davies did not return. The search party mentioned in the intelligence report found a glove in our wire on the left of the salient. On the right of the salient, where the patrol probably had been, a search was made towards the German trenches, but without result.

APPENDIX B

Report on the disappearance of 2/Lieut Crossland and Pte Harvey of the 1 Border Regt whilst on Patrol on the night of 5 - 6.4.16

The patrol was sent out at 21.30 (9.30 pm) by order of Capt Ewbank to patrol for an hour. They left the trenches at Sector Q.10.4 under instructions to return in an hour.

The L/Cpl's (O'Leary) account is that the patrol advanced for about 150 yds & at about 23.45 (11.45 pm) after seeing the German patrol return, moved to the left in search of a shell crater. 2/Lt Crossland left the party when they found themselves obstructed by wire but failed to locate the pit ? & the patrol turned right again. They were searching for the way back when a flare went up. This flare was mistaken for a guiding light and the patrol moved towards it. It was then challenged in English (with a German accent) and then in German. As the patrol was creeping away a second flare went up followed by fire. 2/Lt Crossland was then seen for the last time "standing against the wire".

The survivors worked back by rushes to a crater where they lay till enough light enabled them to see where they were and regain their trench. Pte Harvey was then found to be missing and it is thought he was wounded.

---------- * ----------

READERS NOTE

War records of the German 26th Res Division include a detailed map of the features of the British trenches in sectors Q.10.5 to Q.10.7 which was taken off a captured British officer on 6 April 16. As 2/Lt Crossland was the only officer missing on that particular night, and was patrolling in the vicinity of trench sector in question, it may reasonably be assumed that the map was taken off him. It is astonishing that an officer could be so careless as to take a map of that nature on patrol - his carelessness probably cost many casualties and much grief in the trenches in question.

REPORT ON OPERATIONS WHICH TOOK PLACE ON NIGHT
6th APRIL 1916.

LEFT SECTOR. About 8.50 pm. twelve Germans crept up to ROONEY'S SAP and hurriedly threw into it twelve hand grenades. No damage was done and a burst of rapid fire dispersed the German patrol. This is the incident which was misinterpreted by the observer on the Left Sector as a bombing attack by the first Border Regiment. After the patrol had vanished quiet prevailed for four or five minutes. About 9.0 pm. the enemy artillery opened. Some shells dropped behind HAWTHORNE RIDGE coming from North East direction. Several bits of parapet were blown in at Q.10.3 and the top of FIRST AVENUE was heavily shelled. Trench mortars were very active and wire to the depth of 10 yards was damaged in front of Q.10.3. The K.O.S.B. lines on the left were shelled by a battery from the North East of BEAUMONT HAMEL. The fire was then directed on to the front held by the Border Regiment in the centre. After a short interval another battery opened on the TENDERLOIN and continued for 15 minutes. The range was then lengthened as if our batteries were being searched for.

RIGHT SECTOR.
Shortly before 9.0 pm. a bombing patrol of one Officer and seven men was sent out down the sap in Q.16.6, with a view to finding out if the Germans were patrolling up the dead ground about 50 yards in advance. They reported that a German patrol was moving along in extended order in front. The patrol waited some time to verify this and then retired to report. During this period there was some bombing and firing up the line to the North. The patrol got

(2).

got in just as the bombardment commenced. The whole front of the line held by the South Wales Borderers was subjected to a heavy fire with minenwerfer, H.E. and shrapnel. The greatest concentration appears to have been in the sector Q.16.3-8 and on the communication trenches leading up to it. A strip of wire about 50 yards wide in front of Q.16a.3-6 was entirely levelled and front trenches blown in. At 9.10 pm. the range was lengthened on to the support and communication trenches and a party of Germans entered the front trench. A party of two Officers and some men in support trenches were about 10 yards down BOND STREET from the fire trenches. Someone was heard approaching and the leading officer called out to know who it was, thinking it was one of our men retiring from the front trench. The reply was a shower of hand grenades and bombs. The advacning Germans were heavily fired upon and retired. As soon as the bombardment ceased half the reserve company was pushed up. It was found that the Germans had been in the right half of the left Company. The trench was strewn with unexploded stick grenades, two German hatchets, a dagger, two caps and a coat. Two men were half buried in the fire trench; the Germans pulled one out and took him away as a prisoner. They tried to pull out the other but were apparently unable to do so and left him there. The raiders were wearing broad white bands on both arms. There are four German bodies outside our fire trench which will be brought in to-night.

CASUALTIES.

	Killed		Wounded		Missing	
	Off.	O.R.	Off.	O.R.	Off.	O.R.
Border Regiment		13	1	10		
S.W.Bords.		19	7	31		28
K.O.Bords.	1			1		
M.Gun Coy.		1				
	1	33	8	42	-	28

SIGNALS.   At 9.10 pm. a small stationary light was observed over the enemy's lines.   It was impossible to locate its actual position. This light was not visible after 10.25 pm., which looks as if it was being used in conjunction with the artillery.

signature

Lieut. Colonel, G.S.

7th April 1916.   29th Division.

"A" Form.
MESSAGES AND SIGNALS.

Army Form C. 2121.

Prefix	Code	m.	Words	Charge	This message is on a/c of:		Recd. at	m.
Office of Origin and Service Instructions.			Sent			Service.	Date	
			At	m.			From	
			To					
			By		(Signature of "Franking Officer.")		By	

TO	VIII Corps.	31 DV	36 DV
Sender's Number.	Day of Month	In reply to Number	AAA
* G A 81.	7		

At about 9.45 last night enemy heavily shelled the right Sub Section AAA Whole of front line and communication trenches more or less filled in AAA Enemy were seen crawling forward N. Side of MARY REDAN they were at once bombed AAA Left of right sub section [illegible] on North Side of Salient PICCADILLY – CONSTITUTION HILL and KNIGHTS BRIDGE received most shelling AAA. All wires were cut and trenches made impassable AAA. Enemy is reported to have entered trench but was at once driven out again.

From				
Place				
Time				

The above may be forwarded as now corrected. (Z)

Censor. Signature of Addressor or person authorised to telegraph in his name.
* This line should be erased if not required.

"A" Form.
MESSAGES AND SIGNALS.

Army Form C. 2121.

* G.A 81 (Continued) AAA

A detailed report will be forwarded as soon as possible AAA. Casualties not known exactly but 15 killed and 28 wounded have been reported including 5 Officers AAA Shelling ceased about 11.15 pm the situation now appears to be normal.

Addressed VIII Corps repeated 31 and 36 Divs.

From Place: 29° Div
Time: 5.35.

(2) M. Armstrong Capt.

"A" Form
MESSAGES AND SIGNALS.
Army Form C. 2121.

Prefix	Code	m.	Words	Charge	This message is on a/c of:	No. of Message
Office of Origin and Service Instructions.						Recd. at ___ m.
			Sent			Date
			At ___ m.		Service.	From
			To			
			By		(Signature of "Franking Officer.")	By

TO: VIII Corps

Sender's Number.	Day of Month	In reply to Number	
G.702	7th		AAA

Refer my G.A.81 and your 1.G.98 the total casualties last night were killed Officers 1 Other Ranks 32 wounded Officers 9 other Rks 42 Missing Other Rks 28 total 112 AAA of the missing one man is known to have been taken prisoner in a dug-out Many are probably buried in the débris AAA some have since been dug out but no report as to numbers yet to hand AAA Written report follows AAA.

From: 29th Div
Place:
Time: 3.50 p.m.

"A" Form.   Army Form C. 2121.
MESSAGES AND SIGNALS.

Priority

TO: 8th Corps, 31st and 36th Divns

Sender's Number: G.715   Day of Month: 9.   AAA

At 1530 party of about 200 13th Yorks & Lancs marching on road W of AUCHONVILLERS were shelled otherwise situation normal AAA [illegible] mild N.W wind addressed 8th Corps 31st and 36th Divns.

From: 29th Divn
Place:
Time: 5.7 p.m.

App. III

1 -

                  "off" OR.   H.
Totals. 65/5 · 1562 · 770
_____

27 · 624 .   726
         37   35
       1000   755
       ─────
       1661

Appendix III

Previous copies to be destroyed.

SECRET.

VIII Corps.

G. 282.

POSITION OF HEADQUARTERS.

VIII CORPS.

7th. April, 1916.

VIII Corps.	MARIEUX.
29th Division.	ACHEUX. 13/4/16.
86th Brigade.	~~ACHEUX.~~ MAILLY MAILLET
87th Brigade.	~~MAILLY MAILLET.~~ LOUVENCOURT
88th Brigade.	~~LOUVENCOURT.~~ ENGLEBELMER
31st Division.	BUS LES ARTOIS.
92nd Brigade.	BERTRANCOURT.
93rd Brigade.	BUS LES ARTOIS.
94th Brigade.	COLINCAMPS.
48th Division.	COUIN.
143rd Brigade.	LA HAIE (sheet 57.D. - J.6.b.)
144th Brigade.	SAILLY AU BOIS.
145th Brigade.	SAILLY AU BOIS.

H.Q., VIII Corps.
7th. April, 1916.

W. Buttiver B.G., G.S.
VIII Corps.

36th Division	HARPONVILLE.
Brigade	VARENNES (moving to MARTINSART)
Brigade	PUCHEVILLERS.

SECRET.   Copy. NO... 25 ...

29th Division Order No. 28.

Ref. 57.D. Map.   10th April 1916.
1/40,000

1.   The 86th Brigade will relieve the 87th Brigade in the front line trenches on the nights of the 12/13 and 13/14, and the 87th Brigade will replace the 88th Brigade as Corps Reserve Brigade.

    The 86th Brigade will take over the command of the front line on the night of the 13/14 and will report time of taking over to these Headquarters.

    The 88th Brigade will move into the area ENGLEBELMER – MAILLY MAILLET – BEAUSSART on the above nights, and will establish its Headquarters at ENGLEBELMER on the night of the 13/14th.

2.   The moves will be carried out in accordance with the attached march tables "F" and "G".

3.   The 87th Field Ambulance and the Divisional Train will move from BEAUSSART and RAINCHEVAL to LOUVENCOURT on the 13th and 14th inst. respectively.

4.   Brigades will report to these Headquarters their dispositions in the front line and in billets by 10 a.m. on the 15th inst.

                                                       P. Fuller
                                                       Lieut Colonel, G.S.
Issued at..... 10.p.m. ..   29th Division.

    Copy Nos. 1 – 3 General Staff.   14 Off. i/c Signals
             4   86th Brigade.   15 O.C., Div. Cyclists
             5   87th Brigade.   16 A.A. & Q.M.G.
             6   88th Brigade.   17 A.P.M.
          7 –11   Headquarters R.A.   18 O.C., Div. Train
            12   Headquarters R.E.   19 A.D.M.S.
            13   O.C Divisional Yeomanry. 20 A.D.V.S.
                     21. D.A.D.O.S.
                     ~~22. 31st Division H.Q. (for information)~~
                     ~~23. 33th Division H.Q. ("   ")~~
                     22. 8th Corps.

Ref. Sheet 57.D. 1/40,000.   MARCH TABLE "F" for APRIL 12th 1916.

Unit.	From	To	via	Remarks.
1 Bn. 86th Brigade.	ACHEUX	Front line	Forceville	
1 Bn. 86th Brigade.	ENGLEBELMER	MAILLY-MAILLET	direct	
1 Bn. 87th Brigade.	Front line.	ACHEUX	(MAILLY-MAILLET (BEAUSSART (BERTRANCOURT.	
1 Bn. 87th Brigade.	MAILLY MAILLET	LOUVENCOURT	Forceville.	
1 Bn. 88th Brigade.	LOUVENCOURT	ENGLEBELMER	Bertrancourt Beaussart road junction P.12.c.82. road junction P.23.d.7.6.	
1 Bn. 88th Brigade.	"	MAILLY MAILLET	... Bertrancourt.	

Note. No troops will move east of the line Bertrancourt - Forceville before 6.30 p.m.

C.B. Fuller
Lieut Colonel, G.S.
29th Division.

Ref. Sheet 57.D.
1/40,000.

MARCH TABLE "G" for April 13th 1916.

Unit.	From	To	Via	Remarks.
1 Bn. 86th Brigade.	ACHEUX	Front line	Forceville	
H.Q. 86th Brigade	ACHEUX	MAILLY	do	
1 Bn. 86th Brigade.	BEAUSSART	Front line	MAILLY Maillet.	
1 Bn. 87th Brigade	Front line	LOUVENCOURT	Mailly Maillet	
H.Q. 87th Brigade.	MAILLY	LOUVENCOURT	Beaussart	
			Bertrancourt	
1st Bn. 88th Brigade.	Front line	ACHEUX	do	
			Mailly Maillet	
			Forceville	
1 Bn. 88th Brigade.	Louvencourt	ENGLEBELMER	Bertrancourt	
			Beaussart	
1 Bn. 88th Brigade.	"	BEAUSSART	Mailly Maillet	
			Bertrancourt.	
1 Bn. 86th Brigade.	Arqueves	Mailly	Mealvillers.	
			Acheux	
			Forceville.	
87th Field Ambulance.	Beaussart	Louvencourt	Bertrancourt.	

Note 1. The Divisional Train will move from RAINCHEVAL to LOUVENCOURT on April 14th.

Note 2. No troops will move East of the line BERTRANCOURT - FORCEVILLE before 6.30 p.m.

C.P. Fuller
Lieut Colonel, G.S.
29th Division.

Previous copies to be destroyed.

SECRET.

VIII Corps.
G.384.

POSITION OF HEADQUARTERS.

VIII CORPS

14th April, 1916.

VIII Corps.	MARIEUX.
<u>29th Division.</u>	ACHEUX
86th Brigade.	MAILLY MAILLET
87th Brigade.	LOUVENCOURT.
88th Brigade	ENGLEBELMER.
<u>31st Division.</u>	BUS LES ARTOIS
92nd Brigade.	COLINCAMPS
93rd Brigade.	BUS LES ARTOIS.
94th Brigade.	BETRANCOURT.
<u>48th Division.</u>	COUIN.
143rd Brigade.	LA HAIE (sheet 57.D. - J.6.b.)
144th Brigade.	SAILLY AU BOIS
145th Brigade	SAILLY AU BOIS.

H.Q. VIII Corps.
14th April, 1916.

W. Ruthven B.G. G.S.
VIII Corps.

36th Division   HEDAUVILLE (June 20th)

107th   HARPONVILLE
108th   MARTINSART Chateau (Hamel Subsector)
109th   MARTINSART (Thiepval subsector)

29th DIVISION DISPOSITIONS AT 10-0 P.M.

on 14th April, 1916.

Divisional Headquarters.	ACHEUX.
Divisional Mounted Troops.	AMPLIER.
R.A. Headquarters.	ACHEUX.
15th Brigade. R.H.A.	MAILLY - MAILLET (2½ Btys. in action)
17th Brigade R.F.A.	ENGLEBEIMER (3 Batteries in action)
147th Brigade R.F.A.	AMPLIER.
132nd How. Brigade.	MAILLY - MAILLET (1 Battery in action)
Divisional Ammunition Column.	ARQUEVES.
H.Q. Divisional R.E.	ACHEUX.
London Field Co. R.E.	ENGLEBEIMER.
Kent Field Co. R.E.	MAILLY - MAILLET.
West Riding Field Co. R.E.	ACHEUX.
Headquarters 86th Brigade.	MAILLY - MAILLET.
Brigade Machine Gun Co.	In line,
2nd Royal Fusiliers.	MAILLY - MAILLET and BAUCHON.
1st Lancs. Fusiliers.)	
1st R. Munster Fusiliers.)	Front line.
1st R. Dublin Fusiliers.)	
87th Brigade Headquarters.	LOUVENCOURT.
Brigade Machine Gun Co.	"
2nd South Wales Borderers.	" "
1st K.O.S. Borderers.	"
1st Border Regiment.	ACHEUX.
1st R. Inniskilling Fusiliers.	ANCHEUX.
88th Brigade Headquarters.	ENGLEBEIMER.
Brigade Machine Gun Co.	"
2nd Hants Regiment.	MAILLY - MAILLET.
1st Essex Regiment.	ENGLEBEIMER.
4th Worcester Regiment.	MAILLY - MAILLET.
1/5th Royal Scots.	BEAUSSART.
Newfoundland Regiment.	ENGLEBEIMER.

Dispositions of 29th Division contd.

87th Field Ambulance	ACHEUX.
88th Field Ambulance.	ARQUEVES.
89th Field Ambulance.	ARQUEVES.
Divisional Sanitary Section.	ACHEUX.
Headquarters Divisional Train.	RAINCHEVAL.
Headquarters Coy. Train.	AMPLIER.
No. 2 Coy. Div. Train.	RAINCHEVAL.
No. 3 Coy. " "	BELLE EGLISE.
No. 4 Coy. " "	RAINCHEVAL.
Mobile Veterinary Section.	ACHEUX.
Supply Column.	BEAUQUESNE.
Divisional Ammunition Park.	

Captain G.S.,

29th Division.

Copy Only

5

29th DIVISIONAL CONFERENCE NO.7.
held on 16th April, 1916.

1. Saluting.   The necessity for saluting must be impressed on all ranks. All cars flying a flag must be saluted, whether the occupant is visible or not, since a flag denotes the presence of a higher Commander.

2. Necessity for Secrecy.   Particular care must be taken in censoring letters, and Officers especially must be cautioned about revealing information, which may be of use to the enemy.

3. Necessity for quick digging.   The necessity for teaching men to dig quickly was pointed out. Each man should be given a task, and Platoons should be allowed to return to their billets on completion of their task.

4. Raids.   The importance of taking measures to counter raids was insisted on. A memorandum on the subject is being issued. Every Battalion should work out a scheme for a raid.

5. Training of Specialists.   Specialists should be organised in each Company i.e. Wire cutting parties (wire breaking rifles have been applied for) wiring parties, revetting parties, snipers, grenadiers, smoke experts, etc.

6. Young Officers.   Young Officers must study " Notes on Trench Warfare" and "Principles in Defence Systems", and Company Commanders should test their Subalterns knowledge of their contents.

7. Policing of trenches.   The necessity for utilising police in the trenches in an attack, to rally the men, was pointed out and Brigades should organise police for this purpose. In order to distinguish the various Brigades, it is intended to attach a tin discs to the backs of all ranks, the shape of the disc varying according to the Brigade.

8. Care of French Property.   Officers must not ride over growing crops and care should be taken to avoid damaging the property of our Allies.

9. Horsemastership.   It is proposed to attach Cavalry Officers to R.A. units in order to temporarily replace R.A. Officers who would thus be available for purely gunnery work.

10. Duplication of Officers.   It is very necessary to train understudies to Staff Officers whether in a Brigade or Division. Officers with temporary commissions should be selected and attached to Brigade Staffs. A report should be sent in on the aptitude of each selected Officer for Staff Work. 1 Officer for G.S. and 1 for Q. Branch will be chosen for attachment to Divisional Headquarters.

11. Loyalty to the Crown.   It is desirable as far as possible to inculcate the idea of loyalty and patriotism in the mind of the men, and every effort should be made to this end.

-2-

12. **Selection of M.G. Emplacements for indirect fire.** The 86th and 87th Brigades will select positions for M.G. emplacements on the left and right flanks respectively, to sweep the enemy's communication trenches leading up to the BEAUCOURT ROAD.

13. **Deepening Trenches.** All trenches in the Support and Reserve lines should be deepened so as to afford from 6 to 7 feet of cover i.e. the bottom of the trench should be 3 feet below the fire step. The profile of communication trenches should be as follows:-

[diagram of trench profile: 6' width at top, 4'/ depth, 3' wide at bottom, 6' total]

C.G. Fuller

Lieut. Colonel, G.S.
29th Division.

18th April, 1916.

SECRET

VIII Corps.
G.426.

29th Division.
~~31st   "~~
~~48th   "~~
~~4th Division (For information)~~
~~"Q"~~
~~G.O.C. R.A. VIII Corps.~~
~~B.G.H.A. C.H.A.~~
~~A.D.A.S.~~
~~C.E.~~

The Corps Commander will hold a conference at Corps Headquarters at ~~11 a.m.~~ 2.15 p.m. on April 19th.

The following officers will attend from each Division -

        G.O.C.
        G.S.O. 1.
        B.G. R.A.
        A.A.& Q.M.G.
        C.R.E.

AGENDA

DEFENCE SCHEME.

1.   Co-operation between Divisions in the Corps and between flank Divisions and Corps on our right and left.

2.   Routes for re-inforcements to occupy posts in Green and Brown lines, and if required to reinforce VII and X Corps.

3.   Defence of villages.

4.   Concrete Machine Gun emplacements.

5.   Necessity for constant patrolling.

OFFENSIVE.

6.   Position of Divisional and Corps Headquarters.

7.   Signal arrangements - Runners, Electric Lamps, Flags, Helios.

                                                      8.

(2).

8. Necessity for establishing Strong Points immediately after successful assault.

9. Traffic circuits and necessity for taking them into use at once. Maps showing these circuits are being prepared and will be issued shortly.

10. Evacuation of Civil population.

11. G.O's.C. to be prepared to give Corps Commander :-

   (a). A general outline of their scheme of attack.

   (b) Actual front they intend to assault.

   (c) Allotment of troops to this front.

   (d) Strength of each ~~wave~~ bound.

   (e) Objective of each ~~wave~~ bound on the understanding that the second objective, i.e. the GRANDCOURT - SERRE ridge is to be captured on the first day.

   (f) Any strong points which they wish the artillery to pay special attention to.

The above information to be in writing.

   (g) A rough trench map should also be prepared showing how the Infantry of each Division will be disposed immediately prior to the assault.

MISCELLANEOUS.

12. Necessity of taking care of French property.

13. King's interest in His troops.

14. *Battle police.*

H.Q. VIII Corps.
17-4-16.

               W. Cuttwer   B.G. G.S.
                                   VIII Corps.

SECRET.   COPY NO. 2

Reference 57.D.
Map 1/10,000
Secret.

29th DIVISION ORDER NO. 29.

17th April 1916.

1. The section of the front line held by the 29th Division from midnight April 18/19th will be divided into two sectors.
   The Right Sector will extend from our present right (the junction of Q.17/11 and Q.17/12) to the junction of Q.10/7 and Q.10/6, and the Left Sector from the latter junction to our present left (Q.4.b.Central).

2. The 88th Brigade, with Headquarters at ENGLEBELMER, will take over the Right Sector from the 86th Brigade on the night of the 18/19th, and will report to these Headquarters, when the transfer is completed.

3. The boundary between the sectors will be LIMERICK JUNCTION, 1st AVENUE, TIPPERARY AVENUE, to Railway (all inclusive to Right Sector) and then along 140 contour to the road joining VITERMONT and MAILLY-MAILLET.

4. The Brigade garrisoning a Sector will be responsible for the defence of the portion of the Yellow Line in its sector. It will also detail one Battalion as Divisional Reserve, and notify the name of the Battalion selected, to these Headquarters.
   The Battalions in Divisional Reserve will in the event of an attack, furnish the garrison for the Green Line in the sector, held by their Brigade.

5. Brigades will report their dispositions to these Headquarters by 6.0 pm. on the 19th inst.

C.G. Fuller
Lieut.Colonel, G.S.
29th Division.

Issued at 12.45 p.m.

Copy No.		
1-3.	G.Staff	
4.	86th Brigade	
5.	87th "	
6.	88th "	
7 - 11.	H.Q., R.A.	
12.	C.R.E.	
13.	O.C. Div. Yeo.	
14.	Off. i/c Signals	
15.	O/C. Div. Cyclists.	
16.	A.A.&.Q.M.G.	
17.	A.P.M.	
18.	O/C. Divisional Train.	
19.	A.D.M.S.	
20.	A.D.V.S.	
21.	D.A.D.O.S.	
22.	8th Corps (for information).	

86th Brigade.
87th Brigade.
88th Brigade.
O.C. Divisional Cyclists.
O.C. Divisional Squadron.
C.R.E.
O.C. Divisional Signals.

In consequence of the division of the front line into two sectors, the following amended Allotment of Work should be substituted for that issued on the 11th inst.

C.G. Fuller
Lieut Col, G.S.
29th Division.

18th April 1916.

Unit.	Work.	Order of importance.	Supervised by
Right and Left Brigades within the limits of their sectors.	Advanced firing line.	1	Bde.
	New Support Line.	1	"
	Dug-outs in support Line.	1	C.R.E.
	Bde Hd.Qrs. in support Line.	3	"
	Light T.Mortar Emplacements.	5	Bde.
	Dug-outs for S.A.A., Grenades, Supplies and water in front line system.	6	C.R.E.
	Heavy T.Mortar Emplacements.	8	"
	Improvements to Green Line.	9	Bde.
Right Brigade.	Communications:- (Uxbridge Road to North Withington. Constitution Hill to Gabion Avenue.)	2	"
	Dug-outs in Redoubt Line for S.A.A., rations and water	7	C.R.E.
	Completion of Redoubt Line.	4	Bde.
Left Bde.	Communications:- (3rd, 4th and 5th Avenues).	2	Bde.
	Auchonvillers Defences.	4	"
	Dug-outs in Auchonvillers for S.A.A., rations and water.	7	C.R.E.
Tunnelling Squads.	Underground communications at Mary Redan and E Street.	1	"
Divl. Cyclists & Divl. Squadron.	Trenches for Signal Communications.	1	Off. i/c Signals
	Divl. N. and S. Observation Posts.		C.R.

29th DIVISION DISPOSITIONS AT 10-0 a.m.

on April, 29th 1916.

Divisional Headquarters.	ACHEUX
Divisional Mounted Troops.	"
R.A. Headquarters.	"
15th Brigade R.H.A.	MAILLY MAILLET
17th Brigade R.F.A.	ENGLEBELMER
147th Brigade R.F.A. and 1 Battery	ENGLEBELMER
132nd How. Brigade.	MAILLY MAILLET
Divisional Ammunition Column.	ARQUÈVES
H.Q. Divisional R.E.	ACHEUX
London Field Co. R.E.	ACHEUX
Kent Field Co. R.E.	ENGLEBELMER
West Riding Field Co. R.E.	MAILLY MAILLET
Headquarters 86th Brigade.	LOUVENCOURT
Brigade Machine Gun Co.	MAILLY MAILLET
2nd Royal Fusiliers.	LOUVENCOURT
1st Lancs. Fusiliers.	ACHEUX
16th Middlesex Regiment.	ACHEUX
1st R. Dublin Fusiliers.	LOUVENCOURT
87th Brigade Headquarters.	MAILLY MAILLET
Brigade Machine Gun Co.	TRENCHES
2nd South Wales Borderers.	MAILLY MAILLET
1st K.O.S. Borderers.	TRENCHES
2st Border Regiment.	TRENCHES
1st R. Inniskilling Fusiliers.	MAILLY MAILLET
88th Brigade Headquarters.	ENGLEBELMER
Brigade Machine Gun Co.	31st DIVISION
2nd Hants. Regiment.	TRENCHES

Dispositions of 29th Division contd.

1st Essex Regiment.	ENGLEBELMER
4th Worcester Regiment.	ENGLEBELMER
~~1/5th Royal Scots.~~	
Newfoundland Regiment.	TRENCHES
87th Field Ambulance.	LOUVENCOURT
88th Field Ambulance.	ARQUEVES
89th Field Ambulance.	ARQUEVES
Divisional Sanitary Section.	ACHEUX
Headquarters Divisional Train.	LOUVENCOURT
Headquarters Coy. Train.	"
No. 2 Coy. Div Train.	"
No. 3 Coy. " "	"
No. 4. Coy. " "	"
Mobile Veterinary Section.	ACHEUX
Supply Column.	BEAUQUESNE
Divisional Ammunition Park.	-----------

SECRET.

> HEADQUARTERS,
> 29th DIVISION.
> No. 69S53
> Date. 19/4/16

86th Brigade.
87th Brigade.
88th Brigade.
C.R.A.
C.R.E.
A.A. & Q.M.G.

    With reference to Division Order No.29, the programme for the reliefs of the Infantry Brigades will be as follows:-

	Apr. 18/19 to 28/29	Apr. 28/29 to 8/9	May 8/9 to 18/19	May 18/19 to 28/29
Right Sector.	88th Bde.	87th Bde.	87th Bde.	88th Bde.
Left Sector.	86th Bde.	88th Bde.	86th Bde.	86th Bde.
In Corps Reserve.)	87th Bde.	86th Bde.	88th Bde.	87th Bde.

    It may not be possible to adhere strictly to this table. *Please fill in on the attached form the proposed relief, as per sample, returning enclosure with your reply.*

                     C. Fuller

                    Lieut. Colonel, G.S.

19th April, 1916.   29th Division.

86th Brigade.
~~87th Brigade.~~
~~88th Brigade.~~
~~G.R.A.~~
~~G.R.E.~~
~~A.A. & Q.M.G.~~

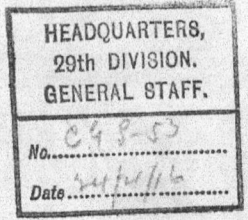

The programme for the reliefs of the Infantry Brigades forwarded in this office C.G.S.53 of the 19th inst. will be amended as follows:-

	April May.	May May.
	28/29 to 8/9	8/9 to 18/19.
Right Sector.	88th Brigade.	87th Brigade.
Left Sector.	87th Brigade.	86th Brigade.
In Corps Reserve.	86th Brigade.	88th Brigade.

24th April, 1916.

Lieut. Colonel, G.S.
29th Division.

Secret

Headquarters,
    VIIIth Corps.

Under cover of an Artillery preparation lasting half-an-hour two raids were made last night on the German Trenches, one by the 87th Brigade at a point just North of HAWTHORN REDOUBT, and one by the 88th Brigade at a point due East of MARY REDAN.

I regret to report both of these were unsuccessful.

In the first raid the party under the command of Captain Byrne, 2nd South Wales Broderers, formed up 50 yards in front of our wire prior to the preliminary bombardment. The enemy's barrage, which replied at once, caused some casualties among the raiders, who then moved forward. The next advance was made 10 minutes before the hour for our Artillery to lift and during this advance several casualties occurred. Captain Byrne reached the enemy's wire with the wire cutting party 5 minutes before the hour arranged, and both he and the next in command as well as several of this party were killed or wounded by shell fire. It is not clear whether this was from shells or trench mortar fire. After further enquiry a special report on this point will be sent in.

At this time the remaining officer finding so many casulaties had occured, decided to retire. No hostile fire except Artillery was encountered. All casualties were carried back, except three who had been blown into the enemy's wire and had not been discovered till daylight; one of these was Captain Byrne the raid Commander.

The casulaties were 24 - of whom 7 were killed.

The 2nd Raid also succeeded in cutting the enemy's wire, but were then met by a determined defence from a party with bombs and machine gun fire from both flanks.

Finding it was not possible to gain the enemy's trenches/

trenches the raiding party fell back according to instructions. One man, who was killed, was left in the enemy' wire after the officer in charge Lieut: Saunders, ~~1st~~ 2nd Hampshire Regiment, had personally ascertained that he was dead.

There was no enemy Artillery fire on the right section of the line; on the left both front and support trenches were much destroyed, and in the 87th Brigade in addition to the 29 casualties among the raiders, there were 69 casualties of which 10 were killed.

Isaac B. de Lisle

30/4/16.

Major-General,
Commanding 29th Division.

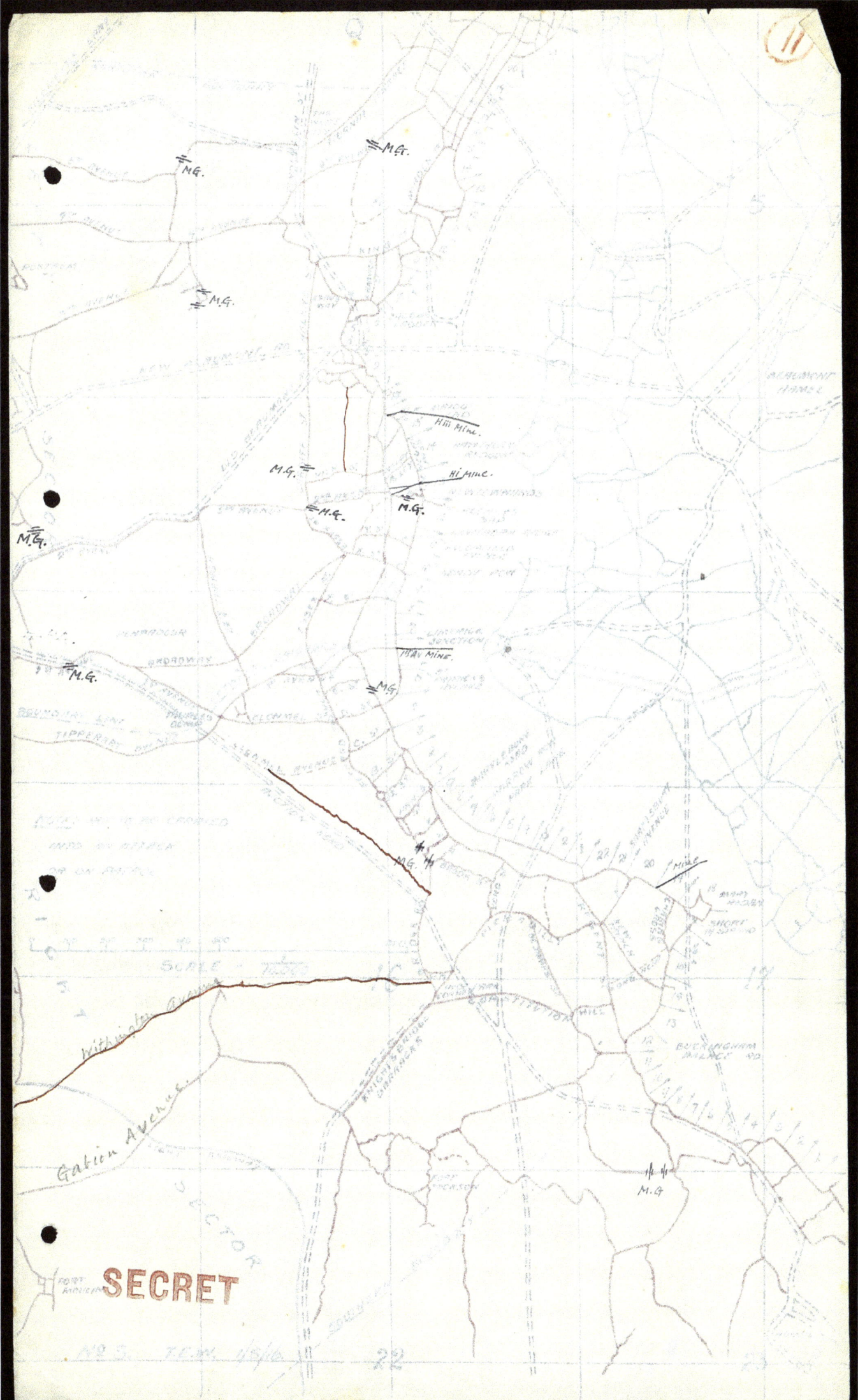

DISPOSITION OF 29TH DIVISION.

April 13th 27th/4, 1916.
After change.

Divisional Headquarters		ACHEUX
Divisional Artillery, R.E. Headquarters		"
86th Brigade.	MAILLY MAILLET AND FIRING LINE	
87th Brigade.	South Wales Borderers	LOUVENCOURT
	Kings Own Scottish Bdrs.	"
	Royal Inniskilling Fus.	ACHEUX
	BORDER REGIMENT	"
88th Brigade	ENGLEBELMER AND FIRING LINE	
	1/5 Royal Scots	BEAUSSART

Divisional Artillery 11 Wagon1 lines BERTRANCOURT, MAILLY, ENGLEBELMER AND ACHEUX

Brigade Ammunition Column and 4 Wagon lines		AMPLIER
Divisional Ammunition Column		ARQUEVES
R.E.	London Company	ACHEUX
	West Riding Company	MAILLY MAILLET
	Kent Company	ENGLEBELMER
R.A.M.C.	87th Field Ambulance	LOUVENCOURT
	88th " "	ARQUEVES
	89th " "	ACHEUX
	Sanitary Section	"
Surrey Yeomanry	*Arrived Acheux 17.4.16*	~~AMPLIER~~
	Divisional Train	LOUVENCOURT
	Divisional Supply Column	BEAUGUESNE
	16th Mobile Veterinary Section	ACHEUX
R.A. HQ		ACHEUX

===============================

SECRET.   Not to be taken in front of
                            Brigade Headquarters.

86th Brigade.
~~87th Brigade.~~
~~88th Brigade.~~
~~C.R.A.~~
~~C.R.E.~~
~~A.A. & Q.M.G.~~

Amendments to "29th Division Defence Scheme".

Delete paras. 4, 5 and 9, and substitute the following:-

4. Division of Line into two sectors.   The section of the front line held by the 29th Division is divided into two sectors.

The Right Sector extends from the junction of Q.17/11 and Q.17/12 to the junction of Q.10/7 and Q.10/8.

The Left Sector extends from the junction of Q.10/7 and Q.10/8 to Q.4.b.Central.

The boundary between the sectors is as follows:

LIMERICK JUNCTION, 1st AVENUE, TIPPERARY AVENUE to Railway (all inclusive to Right Sector) and then along 140 contour to the road joining VITERMONT and MAILLY-MAILLET.

The distribution of the Infantry for defence is as follows:-

Right Sector

	Headquarters at ENGLEBELMER.
Front Line and Supports.	(2½ Battalions (1 Section, Bde.M.G.Co (2 Light T.Mortar Batteries.
Yellow Line.	4 Platoons (one each in Forts, Prowse, Moulin, Withington and Anley.) 1 Section, Bde M.G.Coy.
Brigade Reserve.	1 Battalion less 4 Platoons at ENGLEBELMER. 2 Sections of Bde.M.G.Coy. at ENGLEBELMER.
	Divisional Reserve. 1 Bn. at ENGLEBELMER.

Left Sector.

	Headquarters at MAILLY-MAILLET.
Front Line and Supports.	(2 Battalions.(less one Company.) (2 Light Trench Mortar Batteries. (2 Sections Bde.M.G.Coy
Yellow Line.	1 Company at AUCHONVILLERS. with 1 Section Bde.M.G.Coy.
Brigade Reserve.	1 Battalion. 1 Section Bde.M.G.Coy. at MAILLY-MAILLET.
Divisional Reserve.	1 Battalion at MAILLY-MAILLET.

Divisional Reserve.

2 Battalions as detailed above
13/Yorks. & Lancs.Regt. at MAILLY-MAILLET.
252nd TUNNELLING Coy. at BEAUSSART.

Corps Reserve Brigade.

        2 Battalions billeted at LOUVENCOURT.
        2 Battalions billeted at ACHEUX.
        Brigade Machine Company at LOUVENCOURT.
            (at present loaned to the 31st Division)

5. The Divisional Artillery is divided into two groups, consisting of:-

Right Group.   Headquarters at ENGLEBELMER.

        4 Batteries (18 pdrs-) (one battery not
                         (yet in position)
        1 Battery (4.5" How.)

Left Group.   Headquarters at MAILLY - MAILLET.

        4 Batteries (18 pdrs.) (one battery not
                        (yet in position)
        1 Battery (4.5" Howrs)

In Corps reserve at AMPLIER.

        4 Batteries (18 pdrs.)
        1 Battery (4.5" Hows.)

1 Battery (18 pdr.) has been lent temporarily to 48th Division and 1 Battery (18 pdr.) has been placed at disposal of Corps Heavy Artillery.

6. **Action in case of attack.**

        In the event of an attack, the Brigades on front line will immediately reinforce the garrisons of the Yellow Line up to their full strength as follows:-

Right Sector.

        Fort Prowse.   1 Company and 2 Machine Guns.
        Fort Moulin.   2 Companies and 2 Machine Guns.
        Fort Withington. ½ Company and 2 Machine Guns.
        Fort Anley.   ½ Company and 2 Machine Guns.

Left Sector.

        Auchenvillers
          Village.   1 Battalion and 4 Machine Guns.

        The two Battalions from the Brigades in front line will be sent to garrison the Green Line, and will remain there at the disposal of the Divisional Commander as Divisional Reserve. The 252nd Tunnelling Company in billets will assemble at BEAUSSART and the 13/Yorks and Lancs. Regt. in billets will assemble at MAILLY - MAILLET. They will both report to the Headquarters of the Brigade at MAILLY - MAILLET that they have done so, giving their total strengths available. Instructions as to their disposal will be sent from these Headquarters.

8. **Degree of Readiness.**

        Reserve troops of the Brigade in front line will normally be ready to move at one hours notice, and those of the Corps Reserve Brigade, and Artillery in Corps Reserve at two hours notice. Not more than 25% of the permanent garrisons of the posts mentioned in para.6 are to be employed outside their defensive posts at any one time.

time.

29th Division H.Q.
21st April, 1916.

C.F. Fuller
Lieut. Colonel, G.S.

SECRET.

HEADQUARTERS,
29th DIVISION.
GENERAL STAFF.
No. C.G.S. 71
Date 21/4/16

29th Division.

VIII Corps.
G.471.

When the 4th Division takes over a portion of the front between the 29th and 31st Divisions, the boundary between the 4th and 29th Divisions will be as under, and not as previously arranged.

    Q.4.d.29, Q.4.c.58 – South of 3rd Avenue –
    junction of tracks at Q.2.d.52½ – Railway
    at Q.2.c.80 – Road junction Q.13.b.22 – thence
    as before.

H.Q. VIII Corps.   (Signed) W.RUTHVEN, B.G. G.S.
20th April 1916.   VIII Corps.

-2-

86th Brigade.
87th Brigade.
88th Brigade
C.R.A.
C.R.E.
A.D.M.S.

Forwarded for information.

(Signed)
Lieut Colonel, G.S.
29th Division.

21st April 1916.

Confidential

MESSAGE.

* * *

FROM Lieut-General Sir Aylmer Hunter-Weston, K.C.B., D.S.O.

TO All Officers and Men of the ~~incomparable~~ 29th Division, who took part with him in the historic landing on the Gallipoli Peninsula, 25th April, 1915.

On this, the first anniversary of the landing effected by the incomparable 29th Division near Cape Helles on the Gallipoli Peninsula, I send to each officer and man, who took part in that glorious operation of war, my personal greetings and congratulations on the privilege and opportunity which was accorded to you of being able to do so much for our beloved King and Country.

As fore-shadowed in the personal note I sent to each of you before we landed, you had to face death by bullet, by shell, by mine, by drowning. But nothing deterred either you that are here with me now, or those even more glorious comrades that have gone across the Great Divide and have attained the most noble end that can befall any man. It was your discipline, your training, and your fine esprit-de-corps that enabled you to carry on, notwithstanding your heavy losses, to stick it out, and to win through. You were successful in all the many engagements we fought together on the South end of the Peninsula, and the fact that our troops subsequently evacuated the Peninsula in no way dims the glory of your achievements. Indeed, the success of both the evacuations were greatly due to your good work.

In the great operations, which must come before this war is won by us, and in which we hope that it may be our good fortune to bear a leading part, I know that the 29th Division may always be relied on to emulate the noble example that it set itself a year ago today. This can only be if the officers and men, who have joined the Division in the past 12 months, determine that their discipline and spirit shall

Telephone this cop[y]

Ref Message down Corps comd.
with these marked confidential.
The Div Comdr. fears that otherwise
a copy may find its way to home
papers & this does not appear
desirable.

D.H.

be of as high an order as that that enabled their predecessors to gain so glorious a place on the Roll of Fame.

I consider myself highly honoured to have the 29th Division under my command, and I look forward to taking part with it again in many a victorious fight.

AYLMER HUNTER-WESTON.
Lt-GENERAL.

Headquarters,
VIII Army Corps.
25th April, 1916.

A852

PROGRAMME FOR CORPS COMMANDER - 25TH APRIL, 1916.

Leave Marieux 1430

Munster Fusiliers will halt 1430 West of
Louvencourt on Louvencourt - Marieux road.

Arrived Louvencourt 1440
(visit S.W.B's, K.O.S.B's, 87th Field Ambulance)

Arrive Mailly Maillet 1505
(visit 86th Brigade and West Riding R.E.)

Arrive Englebelmer 1535
(visit 88th Brigade)

Arrive Acheux 1610
(Royal Inniskilling Fusiliers, Border Regt,
London Field Coy. R.E. and 89th Field Ambulance)

Artillery will conform with times at respective villages.

"C" Form (Duplicate). Army Form C. 2123.
MESSAGES AND SIGNALS. No. of Message

| | Charges to Pay. £ s. d. | Office Stamp. |

Service Instructions. OC

Handed in at _____ Office ___ m. Received ___ m.

TO 29th Divn Q

Sender's Number	Day of Month	In reply to Number	AAA
PM 531	25	319	
Acknowledged			

FROM 86th Bde
PLACE & TIME 1121

"A" Form.
MESSAGES AND SIGNALS.
Army Form C. 212.

Prefix	Code	m.	Words	Charge		No. of Message	
Office of Origin and Service Instructions.			Sent		This message is on a/c of:	Recd. at	m.
			At	m.	Service.	Date	
			To			From	
			By		(Signature of "Franking Officer.")	By	

TO: 57th Bde

Sender's Number.	Day of Month	In reply to Number	
A 320	15		AAA

Corps	Commander	will	arrive	Lawrence 46
view	to day aaa		H	Brother
4	of	the	many	officers
aid	area	as	possible	who
landed	with	him	a	year
ago	at	Hellen	what	Muddy
interfering	with	their	work aaa	
He	will	see	their	at
then	Batt.	HQ aaa	He	will
also	visit	Others	at	1610
and	wishes	as	above	aaa
acknowledge.				

KCMorgan Capt

From: 14th Div
Place:
Time:

The above may be forwarded as now corrected. (Z)
Censor. Signature of Addressor or person authorised to telegraph in his name.
* This line should be erased if not required.
(688-0) —McC. & Co. Ltd., London.— W 14142/641. 225,000. 4/15. Forms C 2121/10.

"A" Form.
MESSAGES AND SIGNALS.

Army Form C. 2121.

Prefix	Code	m.	Words	Charge	This message is on a/c of:	Recd. at	m.
Office of Origin and Service Instructions.			Sent			Date	
			At	m.	Service.	From	
			To			By	
			By		(Signature of "Franking Officer.")		

TO 86 Bde   88th Bde

Sender's Number.	Day of Month	In reply to Number		AAA
*A 319	25			

From 29 Div

Place

Time

The above may be forwarded as now corrected.   **(Z)**

Censor.   Signature of Addressor or person authorised to telegraph in his name.
*This line should be erased if not required.
(688-9) —McC. & Co. Ltd., London.— W 14142/641. 225,000 4/15. Forms C 2121/10.

VIII Corps.
G. 528

29th Division.

In confirmation of telephone conversation, the Corps Commander would like to see this afternoon, as many men as possible of the 29th Division who landed with him at CAPE HELLES a year ago, without unduly interfering with their work.

He will see them at their respective Battalion Headquarters.

Will you kindly arrange a programme and forward details to this Headquarters. The Corps Commander will leave here at 2.30 p.m.

H.Q., VIII Corps.
25th April, 1916.

W.F. Dobbie
Capt ----------- B.G., G.S.
VIII Corps.

A

TRANSCRIPT OF MESSAGE TO VIII CORPS

From 29th Div

25 April 16. In reply to G528

Programme as follows. Munster Fusiliers will halt 1430 West of Louvencourt on Louvencourt Masieux road. Arrive Louvencourt 1440 visit two Batt'ns 87 th Bde and Field Ambulance. Arrive Mailly-Maillet 1505 visit 86th Bde and West Riding Field Company RE. Arrive Engelbelmer 1535 visit 88th Bde. Arrive ACHEUX 1610 visit two Batt'ns 87th Bde London Field Company and 89th Field Ambulance.

"A" Form.
MESSAGES AND SIGNALS.
Army Form C. 2121.

Prefix	Code	m.	Words	Charge	This message is on a/c of:	Recd. at	m.
Office of Origin and Service Instructions.			Sent		Service.	Date	
			At	m.		From	
			To			By	
			By		(Signature of "Franking Officer.")		

TO VIII Corps

Sender's Number.	Day of Month	In reply to Number	
* A 322	25	G 510	AAA

Programme aaa from aaa
Münster Fos. aaa halt 1430
West of Louvencourt — Louvencourt
Louvencourt Road aaa Arrive Louvencourt
1440. Visit two Batt's 87th Bde
and Field Ambulances aaa Arrive
Mailly – Maillet 1505 visit 98th
Bde aaa West Riding Field
Company R.E. aaa arrive Engelbelmer
1535. Visit 98th B'n aaa Arrive
ACHEUX 1610 visit two Batt's
87th Bde London Field Company
R.E. and 89th Field Ambulance aaa

H.C. Bryan Capt.

From	29th 21st		
Place			
Time			

The above may be forwarded as now corrected. (Z)

Censor.   Signature of Addressor or person authorised to telegraph in his name.
* This line should be erased if not required.

"A" Form.
Army Form C. 2121.
MESSAGES AND SIGNALS.

Prefix....Code....m.	Words	Charge	This message is on a/c of:	Recd. at....m.
Office of Origin and Service Instructions.				Date....................
	Sent		....................Service.	From....................
Priority	At....m.			
	To		(Signature of "Franking Officer.")	By......................
	By			

TO: 1st H.E.

Sender's Number.	Day of Month	In reply to Number	A A A
A321			

[handwritten message, partially legible:]
... Lowencourt — buses ... M.O. ... send ... on West ... Lowencourt ... arranged ... telephone ...

W.C. Morgan Capt.

From 29 Div.
Place
Time

"C" Form (Duplicate).
MESSAGES AND SIGNALS.

Army Form C. 2123
No. of Message

Charges to Pay. | Office Stamp
£ s. d.

Service Instructions. ZHG

Handed in at .... Office 1210 m. Received 1221 m.

TO 29th Division

Sender's Number	Day of Month	In reply to Number	AAA
S1210	25	A 320	

Message received

FROM
PLACE & TIME   87th Bde

GENERAL STAFF

29th DIVISION

M A Y   1 9 1 6

Appendices attached 1 to 15.

    Operation Orders.
    Conferences.
    Disposition returns.
    Daily Summary of Operations.

Confidential

Duplicate

War Diary
General Staff
29th Division
For the month of
May 1916.

Volume XV

Army Form C. 2118.

WAR DIARY - GENERAL STAFF, 29TH DIVISION.

or

~~INTELLIGENCE SUMMARY~~

(Erase heading not required.)

Instructions regarding War Diaries and Intelligence Summaries are contained in F. S. Regs., Part II and the Staff Manual respectively. Title pages will be prepared in manuscript.

1916.

Place	Date	Hour	Summary of Events and Information	Remarks and references to Appendices
	1st May		A quiet day. G.S.O.3 visited Right Sector of trenches. G.S.O.2 visited M.G. emplacements of 86th Brigade Machine Gun Company. At 8.30 p.m. the enemy bombarded MARY REDAN and our Centre with field guns and minenwerfer but did no damage, a few Germans came up to our wire at MARY REDAN but were promptly driven off. Our casualties were M 3 killed and 6 wounded. 1/2nd Monmouth Regt. arrived as Pioneer Battalion and were billeted in BEAUSSART.	
	2nd May		G.S.O.1 went to see Brig.Gen. Burnett-Stuart at G.H.Q. to get information on various points that occurred during the LOOS Offensive. The Army Commander came to see the G.O.C. at 2.3 p.m.	
	3rd May		G.S.O.2 visited the trenches of the left sector. G.S.O.3 also visited the trenches in the evening. The 1/2nd Monmouths commenced work on a new road through ACHEUX WOOD to ENGLEBELMER (later named "ROTTEN ROW"). The 87th and 88th Brigades changed places in the line, the former taking over the right sector, the latter the left sector during the night 3/4th.	
	4th May		The G.O.C. inspected the M.G. emplacements in the left sector, in the morning. Artillery activity on both sides during the day. A patrol under Lieut. WINTER, Worcester Regt. went out from the left sector during the night, May 3/4th and located a German standing patrol apparently entrenched in the SUNKEN ROAD about point Q.4.d.45.40. they were bombed and fired on but returned without casualty. A list of honours and decorations appeared in the "GAZETTE" dated May 2nd. Lt.Col. Fuller (G.S.O.1) was gazetted Brevet Lt.Col. and many other officers of the Division received honours. *YSO inspected Redoubts*	
	5th May		A demonstration of the use of the Ayrton Fan was given near BUS, the G.O.C. and G.S.O.3. attended. The Corps Commander inspected the 16th Middlesex Regt. at ACHEUX at 10.45 a.m. G.S.O.2 visited the various positions of the battle stragglers posts about ENGLEBELMER and MAILLY-MAILLET accompanied by the A.P.M. G.S.O.3 visited the bombing ground at /LOUVENCOURT	

Army Form C. 2118.

WAR DIARY or INTELLIGENCE SUMMARY

GENERAL STAFF, 29TH DIVISION.

Instructions regarding War Diaries and Intelligence Summaries are contained in F.S. Regs., Part II and the Staff Manual respectively. Title pages will be prepared in manuscript.

(Erase heading not required.)

1916.

Place	Date	Hour	Summary of Events and Information	Remarks and references to Appendices
	5th May		(continued) LOUVENCOURT and inspected the cable trenches at MAILLY-MAILLET. Disposition of 29th Division on this date attached.	Appendix 1.
	6th May		G.O.C. visited 87th and 88th Brigades. G.S.O.2 visited right sector trenches inspecting M.G. emplacements, he also inspected the caves under ENGLEBELMER Church, they would probably accommodate 2 Companies of Infantry. G.S.O.3 visited left sector trenches and M.G. emplacements. Capt. STIRLING COOKSON came to Divisional Headquarters as understudy to G.S.O.3. 1 Officer and 1 man of 88th Brigade were reported missing from a patrol sent out during the night 5/6th to reconnoitre SUNKEN ROAD opposite left sector.	
	7th May		Enemy's Artillery was more active during the day and at night, the 87th Brigade in the right sector lost 3 killed and 7 wounded besides 3 men gassed by gas shells. A Divisional Conference was held at Divisional Headquarters at 11 a.m. A statement of the resulting discussion is attached as Appendix 2. Major Magniac, 1st Lancs. Fus., Lt-Col. Johnson, 2nd Royal Fus., and Lt-Col. Marriott-Smith, R.F.A. attended a Senior Officers' Course at FLIXECOURT.	Appendix 2.
	8th May		G.O.C. rode round the gun positions of the Right Group during the morning. The G.S.O.1 visited AUCHONVILLERS with a view of selecting strong points and a in the village. G.S.O.2 visited the "fort line" especially looking at the M.G. emplacements. The first course of the 29th Divisional School commenced. The 86th Brigade relieved the 88th Brigade in the left sector during the night 8/9th May. A quiet day.	Appendix 3.
	9th May		G.O.C. visited the right sector. G.S.O.2 inspected the deep dug-outs in the left sector. G.S.O.3 and the A.P.M. went round the trenches to select places for battle police posts. It rained most of the day. The enemy's Artillery was rather active against our left sector during the day. Programme of Training being carried out by the Division was this day submitted to VIIIth Corps in accordance with instructions received (Appendix 4).	Appendix 4.

WAR DIARY - GENERAL STAFF - 29TH DIVISION.

or

~~INTELLIGENCE SUMMARY.~~

(Erase heading not required.)

Army Form C. 2118.

1916.

Instructions regarding War Diaries and Intelligence Summaries are contained in F.S. Regs., Part II. and the Staff Manual respectively. Title pages will be prepared in manuscript.

Place	Date	Hour	Summary of Events and Information	Remarks and references to Appendices
	10th May.		The G.O.C. visited "Fort Jackson" in the right sector. G.S.O.1 accompanied the C.R.A. round the trenches to select positions for the guns of a Heavy T.M. Battery. At 4 p.m. the Commander-in-Chief visited the Division, Brigadiers and Staff were introduced to him. He left at 5 p.m. The 1/2nd Monmouth Regiment were all quartered under canvas in MAILLY WOOD. The 4th Worcester Regt. moved from ACHEUX to huts in MAILLY WOOD. Disposition of the Division on this date attached (Appendix 5)	Appendix 5
	11th May.		The G.O.C. visited the northern observation post and the left sector. G.S.O.2 visited the right sector and inspected saps with a view to placing Stokes Mortars in them to shell the enemy's second line. The Corps Commander inspected the Divisional Squadron (Surrey Yeomanry) at 3 p.m. at ACHEUX. A fairly quiet day. Our aeroplanes were heavily fired on by hostile Machine Guns during the morning.	
	12th May.		The G.O.C. visited the Centre trenches and the mines in the centre of our line. G.S.O.3 visited right sector and mine at MARY REDAN; the latter is now 170 feet long. G.S.O.1 attended a conference at Corps Headquarters at 2.30 p.m. G.S.O.1 went round the left sector trenches at night. The enemy's Artillery was very active during the day especially against our right sector. 14 heavy shells were also fired at the BOWERY.	
	13th May.		The G.O.C. visited the right sector trenches. G.S.O.2 visited the right Divl. O.P. and a site for a Corps O.P. also the M.G. emplacements on our extreme right, the latter though open emplacements have an excellent field of fire sweeping the front of MARY REDAN.	
	14th May.		A quiet day.	
	15th May.		G.O.C. visited the right sector trenches and Fort Jackson. G.S.O.1 visited AUCHONVILLERS defences. G.S.O.3 and Capt. Hardress-Lloyd (A.D.C.) went on 8 days leave. It rained all the morning. Col. Palk came to command 2nd Hampshire Regt. but exchanged with Major Middleton (commdg. 1st Bn. Hampshire Regt. 4th Divn.) Operation Order No.15 received from 31st Division giving particulars of reliefs being carried out by them (Appendix 6)	Appendix 6

Army Form C. 2118.

WAR DIARY – GENERAL STAFF, 29TH DIVISION.

INTELLIGENCE SUMMARY.

(Erase heading not required.)

1916.

Instructions regarding War Diaries and Intelligence Summaries are contained in F. S. Regs., Part II. and the Staff Manual respectively. Title pages will be prepared in manuscript.

Place	Date	Hour	Summary of Events and Information	Remarks and references to Appendices
	16th May		The G.O.C. visited the trenches of the right Battalion in the left sector. G.S.O.2 visited the centre of the line. Capt. Cookson visited the Battalions at training. During the night 15/16th May a heavy bombardment was heard some distance north of our line (it was afterwards reported to be against the 48th Division front.) Our front was shelled a little, and fearing a possible attack our Artillery placed a barrage on the enemy trenches opposite our left sector, but no attack materialised.	
	17th May		The G.O.C. visited left sector, inspecting the T.M. battery, emplacements and Artillery F.O. Posts. G.S.O.1 visited the left sector also, inspecting the light railway between 4th and 5th Avenues. G.S.O.2 visited the Reserve Brigade (88th) at training.	
	18th May		The G.S.O.2 visited the left sector and the Northern observation Post in the morning. In the afternoon the G.O.C. showed 86th Brigade where he wished a new trench dug from APPLE TREES to the commencement of 5th AVENUE facing North. A quiet day. An officer of the Lancs. Fus. was reported missing. He went out with a patrol to the SUNKEN ROAD during the night and was fired on early this morning by a German post, one other officer was wounded.	Appx. 7
	19th May		The 88th Brigade relieved the 87th Brigade in the right sector on the night 18/19th. (Appendix 7) The G.O.C. visited the right sector and planned out a new support trench; in the afternoon he inspected the Train at LOUVENCOURT. Capt. Cookson visited the trenches in the right sector by night. During the night 19/20th the enemy tried to surround our standing patrol in the SUNKEN ROAD but was driven off. There were no casualties. [illegible] Border Regt practice with LOUVENCOURT Disposition of the Division on this date attached. (Appendix 8)	Appx. 8

Army Form C. 2118.

WAR DIARY — GENERAL STAFF, 29TH DIVISION.

or

INTELLIGENCE SUMMARY

(Erase heading not required.)

1916.

Instructions regarding War Diaries and Intelligence Summaries are contained in F.S. Regs., Part II. and the Staff Manual respectively. Title pages will be prepared in manuscript.

Place	Date	Hour	Summary of Events and Information	Remarks and references to Appendices
	20th May.		The G.O.C., G.S.O.1, and C.R.A. and 40 officers from the Division witnessed the demonstration at FLIXECOURT at the end of the school course, the G.O.C., C.R.A. and Div.T., T.M. Officer then went to VALHEUREUX to see some T.M. pits, etc. G.S.O.2 visited the right O.P. and Fort Jackson. Major Cripps was appointed Commandant of the Divisional School vice Major Ellis who returned to command his Battalion.	
	21st May.		The G.O.C. visited the right sector with a staff officer from the 88th Brigade in the morning. G.S.O.1 visited the Fort line in the afternoon and inspected the work done by the 1/2nd Monmouth Regt. Capt. Hardress Lloyd took over Command of the Inniskilling Fusiliers (Col. Pierce having been invalided home). Capt. Gee, Royal Fusiliers, was attached to G.S. vice Capt. Cookson who resumed his duties as Staff Captain, 87th Brigade.	
	22nd May.		The G.O.C. visited the left sector and inspected the newly dug trenches. G.S.O.2 also visited the left sector. The G.O.C. met the G.O.C. 31st Division on new Training Ground between the BUS and LOUVENCOURT in the afternoon. A quiet day; fairly heavy Artillery and Mortar firing took place about 10.30 p.m. on our left, against the 31st Division.	
	23rd May.		The G.O.C., G.S.O.1, G.S.O.2, C.R.A., C.R.E., A.A. & Q.M.G. attended a conference at Corps Headquarters at 10 a.m. Notes by G.O.C. 29th Division and VIIIth Corps attached (Appendix 9). G.S.O.2 visited the centre sector in the afternoon. A Divisional conference was held at 4 p.m. at Divisional Headquarters (Appendix 10)	Appx. 9. Appx. 10.
			/The	

Army Form C. 2118.

WAR DIARY - GENERAL STAFF, 29TH DIVISION.

INTELLIGENCE SUMMARY.

(Erase heading not required.)

Instructions regarding War Diaries and Intelligence Summaries are contained in F. S. Regs., Part II. and the Staff Manual respectively. Title pages will be prepared in manuscript.

1916.

Place	Date	Hour	Summary of Events and Information	Remarks and references to Appendices
	23rd May		(continued) The 88th Brigade M.G. Coy. loaned to the 51st Division was relieved from duty on this date with 51st Division and rejoined the 29th Division. (vide 51st. Division Operation Order No.19) Appendix 11. *A quiet day*	Appx. 11
	24th May		The G.O.C. and G.S.O.2 visited the Southern Divisional observation post and the new reserve trench along the right and centre sectors. It rained all the afternoon. A demonstration in wire cutting by Bangalore torpedoes was given on the Divisional bombing ground in the afternoon. The G.O.C. inspected the Divisional School at guard mounting exercises. The G.S.O.3 returned from leave.	
	25th May		The G.O.C. visited the two Brigade Headquarters. G.S.O.1 went along the new reserve trench with Captain Gee. G.S.O.2 took the Second in Command of the 1/2nd Monmouth Regiment to show him work to be done in BROCKS BENEFIT Trench, the southern boundary of the 29th. Division was fixed and a board put up. The G.O.C. and selected Officers and N.C.O.'s went to VALHEUREUX to witness a demonstration in Light Trench Mortar firing, but owing to an accident with the ammunition, the demonstration was postponed. The A.A. & Q.M.G. went on leave.	
	26th May		The G.O.C. and G.S.O.1 attended a Corps conference at 10 a.m., G.O.C.'s notes attached.(Appx.12) The G.O.C. afterwards went to HESDIN to witness a demonstration of Light Trench Mortars. G.S.O.2 went to a demonstration in Machine Guns and Trench Mortars at the French School at Sains - en - Armenois. A quiet day.	Appx.12

Army Form C. 2118.

WAR DIARY — GENERAL STAFF, 29TH DIVISION.

or

INTELLIGENCE SUMMARY

(Erase heading not required.)

Instructions regarding War Diaries and Intelligence Summaries are contained in F.S. Regs., Part II. and the Staff Manual respectively. Title pages will be prepared in manuscript.

1916.

Place	Date	Hour	Summary of Events and Information	Remarks and references to Appendices
	27th May.		The 1st course of instruction at the Divisional School finished. The G.O.C. inspected Officers and N.C.O.'s at 10 a.m. G.S.O.2 visited the Machine Gun emplacements in the right sector with the 88th Brigade Machine Gun Company Commander. G.S.O.2 visited the right sector by night and saw the right machine gun do some night firing against the enemy's first and second line of trenches opposite THIEPVAL WOOD. G.S.O.3 visited the left sector during the morning. The G.O.C. visited the YELLOW LINE in the afternoon.	
	28th May.		A quiet day. A few shells were dropped immediately East of ACHEUX WOOD in the early morning. G.S.O.1 visited the Northern Divisional Observation Post. G.S. took over direction of working parties of Monmouths and Reserve Brigade.	
	29th May.		The 87th Brigade relieved the 88th Brigade in the right sector on the night 28/29th. (Appx.13) The G.O.C. G.S.O.1 and C.R.A. attended a Corps conference at 8 a.m. G.O.C. and G.S.O.2 went to see two Brigades of 4th Division carry out an attack scheme on flagged enemy trenches at YVRENCHES. Enemy shelled main road N.E. of ACHEUX Station at intervals during the morning. One mule was killed, two men slightly wounded. Operation Order No. 27 regarding reliefs being carried out by 36th Division received. (Appx. 14)	Appx.13. Appx.14
	30th May.		The G.S.O.2 went to Corps Headquarters to discuss the proposed raid in conjunction with the other Divisions of the VIIIth Corps. Capt. Gee visited the trenches in the morning. A Divisional conference was held at Divisional Headquarters at 4 p.m. to discuss the arrangements for the coming offensive; Brigadiers, Brigade Majors, and C.R.A. attended. *In Off.* *Major Jolpill and Captn [?] from the Special Bde. Re [?] on the following offensive operations*	

T2134. Wt. W708—776. 500000. 4/15. Sir J. C. & S.

Army Form C. 2118.

WAR DIARY - GENERAL STAFF, 29TH DIVISION.

INTELLIGENCE SUMMARY

(Erase heading not required.)

1916.

Instructions regarding War Diaries and Intelligence Summaries are contained in F.S. Regs., Part II. and the Staff Manual respectively. Title pages will be prepared in manuscript.

Place	Date	Hour	Summary of Events and Information	Remarks and references to Appendices
	31st May.		The G.O.C. visited the left sector in the morning. G.S.O.2 visited the left sector and the Medium Trench Mortar emplacements in the afternoon. G.S.O.1 went to see a demonstration of a Boring Apparatus at RIBEMONT. Daily Intelligence Summaries for the month of May are attached (Appendix 15).	Appx. 15.

C.P. Fuller
Lieut.-Colonel, G.S.,
29th Division.

for G.O.C.

Appendix 1

29th DIVISION DISPOSITIONS AT 10-0 P.M.

on 5th May. 1916.

Divisional Headquarters.	ACHEUX.
Divisional Mounted Troops,	"
R.A. Headquarters.	"
15th Brigade R.H.A.	MAILLY-MAILLET.
17th Brigade R.F.A.	ENGLEBELMER.
147th Brigade R.F.A.	"
132nd How. Brigade.	MAILLY - MAILLET.
Divisional Ammunition Column.	ARQUEVES.
H.Q. Divisional R.E.	ACHEUX.
London Field Co. R.E.	"
Kent Field Co. R.E.	ENGLEBELMER.
West Riding Field Co. R.E.	MAILLY - MAILLET.
Headquarters 86th Brigade.	LOUVENCOURT.
Brigade Machine Gun Co.	LEFT SECTOR.
2nd Royal Fusiliers.	LOUVENCOURT.
1st Lancs. Fusiliers.	ACHEUX.
16th Middlesex Regt.	"
~~1st R. Munster Fusiliers.~~	
1st R. Dublin Fusiliers.	LOUVENCOURT.
87th Brigade Headquarters.	ENGLEBELMER.
Brigade Machine Gun Co.	IN THE LINE.
2nd South Wales Borderers.	RIGHT SECTOR.
1st K.O.S. Borderers.	ENGLEBELMER.
2st Border Regiment.	"
1st R. Inniskilling Fusiliers.	RIGHT SECTOR.
88th Brigade Headquarters.	MAILLY-MAILLET.
Brigade Machine Gun Co.	31st Division.
2nd Hants. Regiment.	MAILLY - MAILLET.

Dispositions of 29th Division contd.

1st Essex Regiment.	LEFT SECTOR.
4th Worcester Regiment.	" "
Newfoundland Regiment.	MAILLY - MAILLET.
Pioneer Battalion. Monmouth.	BEAUSSART.
87th Field Ambulance.	LOUVENCOURT.
88th Field Ambulance.	ARQUEVES.
89th Field Ambulance.	"
Divisional Sanitary Section.	ACHEUX.
Headquarters Divisional Train.	LOUVENCOURT.
Headquarters Coy. Train.	LOUVENCOURT.
No.2 Coy. Divisional Train.	"
No.3 Coy. " "	"
No.4 Coy. " "	"
Mobile Veterinary Section.	ACHEUX.
Supply Column.	BEAUQUESNE.
Divisional Ammunition Park.	

Appendix 2

SECRET.

29th DIVISIONAL CONFERENCE NO.8
Held on 7th May, 1916.

1. **SANITATION.** It does not appear to be realised by Units that they are responsible for the cleanliness of their surroundings even though they may have been left dirty by their predecessors.

2. **DISCIPLINE.** The necessity of pointing out to the Commanding Officers of all units that the appearance of their men on the roads and in billets is the only way the spirit of discipline can be gauged by higher Commanders. That the state of individuals reflects the spirit of unit Commanders. Any further complaints regarding negligence in saluting may necessitate stoppage of leave.

3. **VILLAGE ROAD REPAIRS.** There is an impression that the Field Companies R.E. are responsible for road repairs in villages. This is not so. The senior officer in each village is responsible, and the Town Major acts as his Staff Officer for the purposes of this work.

    Some assistance is required by the Town Major in keeping the villages sanitary, and the roads in repair. Units are responsible for their own billets and the road opposite them, but in practice small working parties are needed and should be provided when asked for.

4. **TELEPHONE.** It was pointed out that in many cases the telephone was used for unimportant messages, when a written message could be sent, and that Staff Officers were often hindered in carrying out their work through having to attend to the telephone. This should be remedied.

5. **CLERICAL WORK.** Endeavours have been made to reduce clerical work to a minimum, and efforts should be continued in this direction.

6. **CARE OF HORSES.** The importance of horsemastership and stable management was pointed out. The recent improvement in exercising horses was commented on.

7. **MINOR ENTERPRISES.** Every Battalion should work out a scheme for a raid. The G.O.C. will from time to time ask Battalions to show him their schemes.

8. **RETALIATION.** The importance of retaliation on the enemy's Artillery was pointed out. A moral superiority over the enemy's Artillery should be established.

9. **LESSONS FROM VERDUN ATTACK.** Copies have been circulated to Brigades. Attention is drawn to the paragraphs regarding defensive organisations, the construction of fire trenches, and the maintenance of communications.

    Battalions should continue the training of their signallers in visual signalling.

    Attention is also directed to the paragraph regarding the moral factor, and especially to the last sentence thereof, i.e.,
    "Self sacrifice of the individual is the essence of victory."

10. **SCOUTS.** The training of Brigade and Battalion Scouts should be carried out on the lines laid down in VIII Corps I.G.203, and the numbers trained should approximate to the establishment laid down in para /

para: 8 of the Corps memo.

It is essential that scouts should know every inch of the ground over which we are operating.

11. TOOLS. Calculations re tools, material, etc. to be carried by Battalions in offensive operations will be based on a "fighting" strength of not more than 800.

It is proposed that 50% of the men should carry tools. These should be slung across the back, and secured with a cord, which could easily be loosened.

12. S.A.A. It was considered that 120 rounds per man would suffice the leading companies in an assault.

13. WATER. Dumps of water in tins will be made to facilitate the supply of water up to the furthest objective. It is also intended to convey water across "No Man's Land" by means of a hose-pipe carried through a tunnel.

14. REVERSING A CAPTURED TRENCH. The best means of reversing a captured trench would appear to be to cut a fire step in the parados. Experiments in this, and also in crossing trenches, should be carried out. The question of removing sections of wire from one side of a hostile trench to the other is also worthy of attention.

15. SHRAPNEL-PROOF COVER. It is intended to provide shrapnel proof cover for the support and forward portions of communication trenches as soon as material becomes available. It is considered that trench boards, covered with a layer of sand bags and earth, would provide useful protection.

16. INHABITANTS. It has been decided by higher authority that it is inadvisable to remove the inhabitants from the villages near the firing line.

17. FIELD COMPANY. It was decided that the Section of the Field Company R.E., now with each front line Brigade should be withdrawn and that one sergeant and 8 men from the R.E. should be attached to Brigades in lieu.

18. GRENADES. It was decided to withdraw No.1 Grenade and only to employ Mills No.5 Grenade.

The importance of training troops in the use of German Grenades was pointed out.

19. BREAD RATION. Application has been made for the issue to troops of a full bread ration, instead of partly bread and partly substitute.

20. SUNDAY REST. Sunday is to be observed as a day of rest, at the discretion of Brigade Commanders.

21. STEEL HELMETS. There is no objection to steel helmets being covered with sandbags, so as to avoid observation by the enemy./

enemy.

22. <u>TELEGRAPH CABLE</u>. In view of the existing shortage of telegraph cable, units should exercise economy in its use.

                                                            Lieut:Colonel, G.S.,

10th May, 1916.   20th Division.

AGENDA FOR CONFERENCE ON 7/5/16.

1. <u>Lessons from VERDUN attack.</u> (Copies will be circulated to Brigades.)
   Defensive operations. <u>organization</u> <u>Shelters.</u> 15 feet of earth cover required with 2 or 3 outlets.
   Sentries to be placed in covered niches near dug-outs, and provided with some means for alarming the garrison.
   Supply of tools, grenades and rockets in each shelter.

   <u>Fire Trench</u>, must be continuous, as isolated supporting points are easily located by aeroplanes, and become shell traps.

   <u>Maintenance of Communications.</u> Visual signalling and pigeons should be employed, in addition to telephones and runners.
   School for visual signalling is being established by the Corps, and 5 men per Brigade will attend, commencing on the 9th inst.
   Rockets are the best means of <u>immediate</u> communication.
   <u>Moral Factor</u> has the greatest weight.

2. <u>Use of flags in the offensive.</u> At LOOS, flags were carried by 15th Division during the attack, and proved of great assistance.
   One man per platoon carried yellow flag 2' x 2' on a 3' stick.
   One man per bombing squad carried yellow flag 1' x 1' on a 5' stick.
   In order to mark the progress of their platoons and squads, Flank Divisions carried yellow flags with black cross, and the 1st Division red flags with a white stripe.

3. <u>Patrols.</u> Necessity for them, but number of officers sent out with them to be strictly limited.

4. Calculations re tools, material, etc. carried by Battalions in active operations should be based on a "fighting" strength of not more than 800.

5. Whether the first troops in the assault should carry full complement of S.A.A..

6. Provision of water up to and at "furthest objective".

7. Best method of "reversing" a captured trench, taking into consideration its probable depth.

8. The possibility of providing shrapnel proof head cover for the forward portions of communication trenches.

9. <u>S.O.S. Signal.</u> The best rockets only to be used - rockets to be altered each week.

10. Removal of inhabitants from "forward area".

11. <u>Deep dug-outs.</u> More R.E. and timber required so that work can be pressed on.

12. Organisation of Division, Brigade and Battalion Scouts, Vide VIII Corps I.G. 203.

/13.

13. Withdrawal of Field Company Section from front line work under Brigades. (vide notes on Trench Warfare, para. 24.)

14. Allotment of Monmouth Pioneer Battalion.

15. Withdrawal of No. 1 Grenade, and employment only of Mills Grenade No. 5.
    Establishment of No. 1 Grenade 4000
    "   " No. 5   "   38000
    Troops should be trained to use German grenades.

16. The possibility of the issue of a full bread ration instead of partly bread and partly substitute.

17. The inadvisability of Battalion stores being interchangeable between Brigades.

18. Accommodation in huts in MAILLY, etc.

Appendix 3

SECRET. Copy No. 3

29th DIVISION ORDER NO. 31.

Reference
57D Map 1/10,000.

6th May 1916.

1. The 86th Brigade will relieve the 88th Brigade in the Left Sector on the night 8/9th May, and will report to these Headquarters when the transfer is completed.

2. The 86th Brigade will not move East of the line BERTRANCOURT - FORCEVILLE before 7.0 pm.

3. The 86th and 87th Brigade Machine Gun Companies will remain in the Left and Right Sectors respectively, and will not be relieved.

4. Brigades will report their dispositions to these Headquarters by 12 Noon on the 9th inst.

5. The 88th Brigade, on relief, will be in Corps Reserve.

C.P. Fuller.
Lieut.Colonel, G.S.
29th Division.

Issued at _____

Copy No. 1-3. General Staff   15. O.C.Div. Cyclists.
       4. 86th Brigade   16. A.A. & Q.M.G.
       5. 87th Brigade   17. A.P.M.
       6. 88th Brigade   18. O.C., Divisional Train.
     7-11. H.Q., R.A.   19. A.D.V.S.
      12. C.R.E.   20. A.D.M.S.
      13. O.C. Divl. Yeo.   21. D.A.D.O.S.
      14. Off.I/C Signals   22. 8th Corps (for information).
              23. 31st Division (for information).

Appendix 4 War Diary

G.S.-26
9/5/16

Headquarters,

   VIII Corps.

      Herewith programme of training as requested.

(Sd) D. Ovey.
Capt.
for Lieut.Colonel, G.S.,
29th Division.

9/5/16.

29th DIVISION TRAINING PROGRAMME.

1. Since the arrival of the Division in France, training has been continued, so far as far as circumstances would permit, on the lines laid down at Suez in G.S. Memorandum No. 29 (Vide Appendix A), as modified by the instructions received from VIII Corps.

The programme included marching, musketry, machine gunnery, and grenade throwing. To these were added Lewis Gunnery on receipt of Lewis guns shortly before the departure of the Division for France.

2. The following further arrangements have been made, since arrival in this country.

Instruction of Company Commanders, Young Officers and N.C.Os.
Brigades have been carrying out the instructions of the above, both while in the trenches and while in reserve, in accordance with the programme laid down in VIII Corps G.188.

3. Small Offensive and Defensive Schemes.

Officers commanding Companies and platoons in the line have been instructed to make out small schemes for offence and defence, and to submit them to Battalion Commanders for criticism. These schemes have to include in their scope the Companies or platoons on both flanks.

Necessity for quick digging. This has been impressed on all ranks. Tasks are allotted, and platoons are permitted to return to their billets on completion of their task.

4. Raids.

Battalions have been practising raids and wire-cutting both by day and night. This practice includes revolver shooting. Notes on the preparatory measures for a raid have been issued. Every Battalion in the line has been instructed to make out a scheme for a raid.

5. Consolidation of entrenched positions etc.

Brigades have been specially instructed to include in their training programme :-

    (1). The consolidation of entrenched positions.
    (2). The attack on a part of the line, where the enemy have

have been able to maintain their defence.

6. <u>Attack Practise.</u>   A facsimile of the enemy's trenches on a scale of 1 to 20 is being laid out close to Divisional Headquarters. This has been ~~xxxxxxxx~~ delayed owing to protracted negotiations to obtain a full size ground, which in the end fell through, as the landowners would not consent to surrender their land for the purpose.

7. <u>Scouting.</u>   Units have formed squads for this purpose, practising by day and night.

8. <u>Bayonet Fighting.</u>   Three Army Staff Gymnastic Instructors have been temporarily attached to the Division, and are now training one N.C.O. per platoon in Bayonet Fighting. This subject is also taught at the Divisional School. Practise grounds have been laid out at LOUVENCOURT and ACHEUX.

9. <u>Musketry.</u>   A rifle range near FORCEVILLE is available on Tuesdays, Thursdays and Sundays; on the remaining days of the week it is allotted to the 36th Division. The range has 2 targets, and musketry for the present is confined to the training of bad shots.

10. <u>Machine Gun Company Re-inforcements.</u>   Brigades have been training re-inforcements for their Machine Gun Companies to replace casualties, as it is not certain that re-inforcements from the Machine Gun Corps will be forthcoming when required.

11. <u>Light Trench Mortars.</u>   Re-inforcements for the Brigade Light Trench Mortar Batteries are being trained by the Reserve Brigade at LOUVENCOURT.

12. <u>Lewis Gunnery.</u>   Battalions have been training fresh teams of Lewis Gunners to man the additional 4 Guns per Battalion, (making a total of 8 guns per Battalion), which have been received.

13. <u>Grenadiers.</u>   Two bombing grounds have been laid out, one at ACHEUX and one at LOUVENCOURT. These have been in constant use by the Reserve Brigade. The object aimed at is that every man should have practise in throwing live bombs, and that squads should be trained to work together in clearing hostile communication trenches etc.

14. <u>Rapid Wiring.</u>

(3).

14. <u>Rapid Wiring.</u> Instruction is being given to the Infantry in rapid wiring, in accordance with the method taught at the Fourth Army School.

15. <u>Signalling.</u> Battalions are continuing the training of their signallers, which was in progress in Suez, up to the full establishment of 24 per Battalion. The Infantry Brigades have some 139 efficient signallers and 182 partially trained. A refresher course for signallers is commencing at VIII Corps Headquarters on the 10th inst., and 15 men from the Division are attending.

16. <u>Divisional School.</u> A Divisional School was started at Acheux on the 8th inst, and a class of 13 Officers and 52 N.C.Os (i.e. 1 Officers and 4 N.C.Os per battalion) are now undergoing a three weeks course of instruction.

17. <u>Gas School.</u> All Units have attended a lecture on protection from gas attack and have passed through a gas chamber. Courses of instruction lasting four days, and attended by 11 Officers and N.C.Os., are being held at Louvencourt under the Divisional Gas Officer, and 3 N.C.Os. who have been trained at Fourth Army H.Q. It is intended that at least one N.C.O, per Company throughout the Division and as many officers as possible should undergo the training.

18. <u>Duplication of Officers.</u> Understudies to Staff Officers are being trained at Division and Brigade Headquarters. Officers with temporary commissions are selected and attached to Brigade Staffs.

19. <u>Courses of Instruction.</u> The numbers of Officers and men who have attended, and are now attending special courses of instruction are shewn on attached Appendix B.

App. A

G.S. MEMORANDUM NO.29.

With reference to Conference No.3, paragraph 2, programmes of training should be arranged so as to embrace, in addition to skill at arms, and the ability to carry out ceremonial drill with accuracy and smartness, the following subjects:-

(1) Marching (up to 15 miles with packs and S.A.A.)

(2) Musketry (including field firing of a practical nature)

(III) Machine Gunnery on the range, and the tactical employment of Brigade Machine Gun Batteries.

(IV) Grenade throwing, including the tactical employment of grenadiers in large numbers in attack and defence.

2. Unless marches are intended to be a purely physical exercise or for the practice of march discipline, protective measures must always be adopted.

During halts commanding officers should instruct subordinate officers in minor tactics, by means of small schemes which must be carefully prepared beforehand. These schemes should give a General and Special Idea, on which are based " Situations", suitable for a small unit. Two or three questions can be asked on each " Situation" on the ground. For this purpose it will be found convenient to divide the officers into Syndicates.

3. From 1st March onwards, on his return from leave, the G.O.C. will inspect each Battalion and other units in camp, on parade and at training.

4. Programmes for weeks subsequent to the week ending 12th inst. February will be submitted to these Headquarters by 12 noon on the preceding Saturdays.

(sgd.) C.G.Fuller.
Lieut. Colonel, G.S.
29th Division.

1st February, 1916.

App B.

COURSES OF INSTRUCTION.

COURSES	PLACE.	Already Trained Off.	O.R.	Now in Training Off.	O.R.
Senior Off. Course	FLIXECOURT	3	-	3	-
Ordinary Infy. Course	"	-	-	13	13
Medium Trench Mortar Course	VALHEUREUX	9	99	1	12
-do-	FLIXECOURT	2	-	-	-
Light Trench Mortar Course	HESDIN	1	1	1	-
-do-	VALHEUREUX	5	59	1	11
Heavy Trench Mortar Course	"	1	1	-	-
Machine Gun Course (Vickers)	CAMIERS	1	3	1	4
Lewis Gun Course	"	3	17	-	-
Hotchkiss Gun Course	"	-	2	-	-
Gas Course	Fourth Army H.Q.	4	3	-	-
Junior Artillery School	HAVERNAS	4	3	3	3
Wireless Course	H.Q.	-	6	-	-
Signalling Course	MARIEUX	-	-	-	15
Sniping Course	PONT NOYELLES	-	-	1	8
Instruction in distinguishing between Allies & Hostile aircraft	BERTRANCOURT	4	16	-	-
		37	210	24	66

The Strength of the 88th Brigade is as follows:-

Unit.	Officers.	Other Ranks.
Brigade Headquarters	5	81
4th Worcester Regiment.	27	954
2nd Hants Regiment.	22	843
1st Essex Regiment.	27	981
Newfoundland Regt.	27	945
	103	3723

They have to find the following working parties daily:-

VIII Corps	562	Other Ranks)	Vide detail attached.
C.R.E. 29th Div:	232	" ")	
Digging Cable Trenches	640		
	1434		

Appendix 5

29TH DIVISION DISPOSITIONS AT 10.p.m.
ON MAY 10TH 1916.

Divisional Headquarters.	ACHEUX.
Divisional Mounted Troops.	"
R.A. Headquarters.	"
15th Brigade R.H.A.	MAILLY-MAILLET.
17th Brigade R.F.A.	ENGLEBELMER.
147th Brigade R.F.A.	"
132nd (How.) Brigade.	MAILLY-MAILLET.
Divisional Ammunition Column.	ARQUEVES.
Headquarters Div: R.E.	ACHEUX.
London Field Coy. R.E.	"
Kent Field Coy. R.E.	ENGLEBELMER.
West Riding Field Coy. R.E.	MAILLY-MAILLET.
Headquarters 86th Brigade.	" "
Machine Gun Company.	LEFT SECTOR.
2nd Royal Fusiliers.	MAILLY-MAILLET.
1st Lancs. Fusiliers.	LEFT SECTOR.
1st Royal Dublin. Fusrs.	" "
16th Middlesex Regiment.	MAILLY-MAILLET.
Headquarters, 87th Brigade.	ENGLEBELMER.
Machine Gun Copmany.	RIGHT SECTOR.
2nd S.W.Bs.	RIGHT SECTOR.
1st K.O.S.Bs.	ENGLEBELMER.
1st Border Regiment.	"
1st Innis. Fusiliers	RIGHT SECTOR.
Headquarters, 88th Brigade.	LOUVENCOURT.
4th Worcester Regiment.	MAILLY-MAILLET.
2nd Hants. Regiment.	LOUVENCOURT.
1st Essex Regiment.	ACHEUX.
Newfoundland Battalion.	LOUVENCOURT.

Pioneer Battalion (Monmouth Regt.)	ACHEUX WOOD.
87th Field Ambulance.	ARQUEVES.
88th Field Ambulance.	LOUVENCOURT.
89th Field Ambulance.	ACHEUX.
Divisional Sanitary Section.	ACHEUX.
Headquarters, Divnl: Train.	LOUVENCOURT.
Headquarter Company Train.	LOUVENCOURT.
No.2 Company Train.	LOUVENCOURT.
No.3 Company Train.	LOUVENCOURT.
No.4. Company Train.	LOUVENCOURT.
18th Mobile Vet.Section.	ACHEUX.
Supply Column.	BEAUQUESNE.

Appendix 6

SECRET.   COPY NO. 15

Reference
1/40,000 Map.

31st DIVISION ORDER NO.18

14.5.16.

1. (a) The line held by the Division will be divided into two sectors which will be known as the Right and Left Sector respectively.

   (b) **Right Sector.** From present right (Trench Q.4.16 inclusive) to left of Trench K.29.4 inclusive.

   (c) **Left Sector.** From left of Trench K.29.4 exclusive to present left (Trench K.23.1 inclusive).

   (d) The dividing line between sectors will be junction of trenches K.29.4/5 - S corner MATTHEW COPSE- N corner LA SIGNY FARM Orchard- PYLON AVENUE (1st entrance).

2. The right sector will be held alternately by the 92nd and 93rd Brigades as follows :-

   Bde.H.Q.   -   COLINCAMPS
   2 Battalions -   In Trenches
   1 Battalion   -   COLINCAMPS.   Brigade Reserve
   1 Battalion   -   BUS.   Divisional Reserve.
   Brigades will relieve every 10 days.
   Battalions in Trenches will relieve every 5 days.

3. The left sector will be held permanently by the 94th Brigade as follows:-

   Bde.H.Q.   -   COURCELLES.
   1 Battalion   -   In Trenches
   1 Battalion   -   COURCELLES.   Brigade Reserve.
   1 Battalion   -   BUS.   Divisional Reserve.
   Battalion in Trenches will be relieved every 5 days.

4. The 92nd or 93rd Brigades will, when out of the Trenches, be in Corps Reserve.
   Bde.H.Q.   -   BUS.
   2 Battalions -   BUS.
   2 Battalions -   WARNIMONT WOOD.

5. On the 15th May the 94th Brigade will take over the left sector from the 93rd Brigade.
   All necessary details will be arranged by the Brigadiers concerned.
   Moves to be carried out in accordance with the attached March table.

6. No trench or supporting point will be evacuated until relieved.

7. Reports to Divisional Headquarters when reliefs are complete.

8. 93rd and 94th Brigades will render by 6 p.m. tomorrow evening a statement shewing how the line is held.

Hy. Steinhausehnayer
for Lieut-Colonel
General Staff
31st Division.

31 Div.H.Q.

Issued at 5 pm

Copy No.	
1	92 Inf.Bde.
2	93 Inf.Bde.
3	94 Inf.Bde.
4	31 Div.Arty.
5	31 Div.Signals
6	"A" Branch
7	A.P.M.
8	A.D.M.S.
9	D.A.D.O.S.
10	A.D.V.S.
11	31 Div.Train
12	S.S.O. 31 Div.
13	Office Copy
14	War Diary.
15	29 Div. (for information)
16	48 Div. (for information).

31st DIVISION ORDER NO.16. MARCH TABLE.

UNIT.	FROM	TO.	HOUR OF START.	REMARKS.
92nd Inf.Bde.				
2 Battalions.	BUS.	WARNIMONT WOOD.	9.45 a.m.	
93rd Inf.Bde.				
1 Battalion.	COURCELLES.	BUS.	On relief by Battalion 94th Inf.Bde.	Using road N of BERTRANCOURT via J.27.d.5.4.
94th Inf.Bde.				
1 Battalion.	WARNIMONT WOOD.	Trenches COURCELLES.	2.0 p.m.	{Using Southern road
1 Battalion.	WARNIMONT WOOD.		9.0 a.m.	{through BERTRANCOURT
1 Battalion.	WARNIMONT WOOD.	BUS.	9.45 a.m.	{itself.

Appendix 7   SECRET

SECRET

Copy No. 3

29th DIVISION ORDER NO. 32.

Reference :
57D Map 1/10,000

16th May, 1916.

1. The 88th Brigade will relieve the 87th Brigade in the Right Sector on the night of 18/19th May, and will report to these Headquarters when the transfer is completed. The 87th Brigade on relief will be in Corps Reserve.

2. The 88th Brigade will not move East of the line BERTRANCOURT - FORCEVILLE before 8.0 p.m.

3. The 87th Brigade Machine Gun Company will remain in the Right Sector and will not be relieved.

4. The Brigades will report their dispositions to these Headquarters by 12 Noon on the 19th instant.

C.J. Fuller
Lieut. Colonel, G
29th Division.

Issued at............12.15 p.m.

Copy No. 1-3. General Staff
4. 86th Brigade.
5. 87th Brigade.
6. 88th Brigade.
7 - 11 C. R. A.
12. C. R. E.
13. O.C. i/c Signals
14. O.C. Divl: Cyclists Det:
15. A.A. & Q.M.G.
16. A. P. M.
17. O.C. Divl: Train.
18. A.D.V.S.
19. A.D.M.S.
20. D.A.D.O.S.
21. VIII Corps (For informat
22. 36th Division (do. do

Appendix 8.

29th DIVISION DISPOSITIONS
at 10.0 a.m. on May 19th 1916.

Divisional Headquarters:	ACHEUX.
R.A. Headquarters.	"
15th Brigade R.F.A.	MAILLY-MAILLET.
17th Brigade. R.F.A.	ENGLEBELMER.
147th Brigade. R.F.A.	"
132nd (How.) Brigade.	MAILLY-MAILLET.
Divisional Ammunition Column.	ARQUEVES.
H.Q. Divisional R.E.	ACHEUX.
London Field Coy. R.E.	"
Kent Field Coy. R.E.	ENGLEBELMER.
West Riding Field Co. R.E.	MAILLY-MAILLET.
H.Q. 86th Brigade.	LOUVENCOURT.
M.G. Company.	"
2nd Royal Fusiliers.	"
1st Lancs. Fusiliers.	"
1st R. Dublin Fusiliers.	"
16th Middlesex Regt.	"
H.Q. 87th Brigade.	ENGLEBELMER.
M.G. Company.	(8 Guns in Front & Support Lines (4 " " YELLOW LINE, (4 " " ENGLEBELMER (Res.)
2nd South Wales Bdrs.	LEFT SUB-SECTOR.
1st K.O.S.Bs.	MAILLY-MAILLET WOOD.
1st Royal Innis. Fusiliers.	RIGHT SUB-SECTOR.
1st Border Regiment.	ENGLEBELMER (Bde Reserve.)
H.Q. 88th Brigade.	MAILLY-MAILLET.
4th Worcester Regiment.	IN THE LINE.
2nd Hants Regt.	MAILLY-MAILLET (Bde. Reserve)
1st Essex Regiment.	IN THE LINE.
Newfoundland Battalion.	MAILLY-MAILLET (Divnl. Resve.)
Pioneer Battalion (Monmouth Rgt.)	" "
87th Field Ambulance.	LOUVENCOURT.
88th Field Ambulance.	ARQUEVES.
89th Field Ambulance.	ACHEUX.

- 2 -

Divisional Sanitary Section.
Headquarters Divisional Train.   ACHEUX.
Headquarters Company Train.   "
No. 2 Coy. Train.   "
No. 3 Coy. Train.   "
No. 4 Coy. Train.   "
18th Mobile Vet. Section.   LOUVENCOURT.
Supply Column.
                                        BEAUQUESNE.

Headquarters,
VIII Corps.

    Herewith disposition of formations in 29th Division as called for in your G.167 of 31st March.

                                    Major General.
29th May, 1916.   Commanding 29th Division.

Appendix 9   *War Diary*

CONFIDENTIAL.   VIII Corps.
G. 959.

4th Division.   G.O.C., R.A.
29th Division. C.E.
31st Division. "Q"
48th Division. A.D.M.S.
                15 Sqdn, R.F.C.

The Corps Commander will hold a Conference at Corps Headquarters at 10-0 am. on May 23rd 1916.

The following will attend from each Division :-

G.O.C.
G.S.O. 1.
A.A. & Q.M.G.
G.O.C., R.A.
C.R.E.

O.C., 15 Sqdn., R.F.C.

AGENDA.

(a) Progress in the preparations for the offensive.
(b) Defensive Work.
(c) Training Arrangements.

H.Q., VIII Corps.   W. Rutturen   B.G., G.S.
19th May 1916.   VIII Corps.

29th DIVISION.

(a) OFFENSIVE PREPARATIONS.

1. FRONT LINE SYSTEM.

The work now being done on defensive preparations will also be useful for offensive action. On the Right, a support trench is being made via ST JAMES STREET, BROOK ST. and FETHARD Street, and a reserve trench from FORT JACKSON across CONSTITUTION HILL, along ST JOHN'S Road to CLONMEL Avenue.

On the Left a support trench has been dug parallel to and East of CARDIFF Terrace, from PILK Street North.

A reserve trench has also been dug from 88th trench to LUNA Terrace, and YOUNG Street. This will complete trenches required for offensive work.

2. COMMUNICATION TRENCHES.

The main avenues of approach are now completed.

3. BRIGADE H.Q.

Work is in progress on the three Brigade Battle Headquarters two in UXBRIDGE Road and one in FORT BUCKLEY.

4. DUG-OUTS

Deep dug-outs are under construction as follows:-

	Accomodation ready.	Under construction for additional.	Total.
Right Subsection.	690 men.	490 men	1180
Left subsection.	900 men.	500 men	1400.

When these dug-outs are completed, additional dug-outs will be commenced. The difficulty in obtaining suitable timber, especially 3" sheeting, is somewhat hampering the work.

5. DIVISIONAL O.Ps.

The Northern and Southern Divisional Observation Posts are ready for use.

6. GUN EMPLACEMENTS.

5 18 pdr. Batteries and 3 4.5" How. Batteries in action at present in their battle positions.

7. 18 pdr. Batteries - emplacements under construction, but could be occupied at any time.

O.Ps. Some are in use, and fresh ones are being constructed.

7. ARTILLERY H.Q.   Left Group Headquarters ready and occupied – Right Group advanced position constructed.

8. HEAVY T.M. EMPLACEMENTS.   Positions for these guns selected but emplacements not yet built.

9. MEDIUM T.M. EMPLACEMENTS.   8 emplacements are ready, and 8 more have been selected but not yet built.

10. TUNNELS.   H.III was 893' long on the 21st inst. This is long enough to allow of construction of T.M. emplacements.

    H.I was 552' long on the 21st inst. 200' additional required to allow of construction of T.M. emplacements.

    1st Avenue was 320' long on the 21st inst. 20' additional required to allow of construction of T.M. emplacements.

    MARY was 286' long on the 21st inst. 344' additional required to allow of construction of T.M. emplacements.

    The average advance is now some 15 feet per diem for the Mary Tunnel, so that a minimum of three weeks fro 21st (i.e. till the 14th June) will be required to complete the tunnels.

11. MACHINE GUN POSITIONS.   Emplacements for the Machine Guns of two Brigade Machine Gun Companies have been prepared, and are being provided with over-head cover, as the provision of material will admit. Positions for indirect fire for 6 Groups of Machine Guns are being prepared.

12. CABLE TRENCHES.   The deep trenches for cables will, it is anticipated, be completed by the 28th May. The Dug-outs for Signal personnel will be ready shortly afterwards.

13. FORWARD ROADS.   (a) Road due East from ENGLEBELMER to KNIGHTS – BRIDGE BARRACKS, and then due North. Three bridges finished, one nearly ready, three more bridges to insert.

(b)

(b) AUCTION Road and deviation track to Northeast Road cleared, but three bridges to be made.

(c) OLD BEAUMONT ROAD. Diversion three quarters completed. Three bridges to be made.

(d) NEW BEAUMONT Road. two bridges ready to be inserted

(e) AUCHONVILLERS - MESNIL Road. Bridges not yet commenced.

(f) AUCHONVILLERS - ENGLEBELMER Road. One bridge at Anley Avenue to be strengthened to take motor lorries.

14. DUMPS. The positions of the forward dumps have been selected. Work on them will probably be confined to providing splinterproof cover. The Divisional Dump near AUCHONVILLERS is complete.

(b) DEFENSIVE PREPARATIONS

1. **FRONT LINE SYSTEM.**

    Work is in progress in (i) deepening trenches in firing and support lines, and deepening communication trenches between them, also in making a continuous support line on the right from Q.17.c.11, along ST JAMES' STREET - PICCADILLY - BROCK Street - FETHARD St.; (ii) in completing reserve line from North of FORT JACKSON, St JOHN'S Road, 88th trench, new 86th trench, LUNA Terrace, YOUNG Street to 5th Avenue.

    The wiring of the front, support and reserve lines will be completed.

2. **YELLOW LINE.**

    Work is in progress in clearing out the trench from FORT MOULIN to GABION Avenue, joining it on to FORT WITHINGTON, and cleaning out the trench from the latter to AUCHONVILLERS. Dumps for S.A.A., GRENADES, Rations, Water etc have been made in all the forts, but it has not been possible to dig deep dug-outs in them.

    The line in front of AUCHONVILLERS has been cleaned out, and a strong point made just North of the ~~Old~~ New BEAUMONT Road. Two other strong points, one in the centre, and one at the South end of the village will be made.

    A trench is being dug along Observation Hedge from 5th Avenue Northwards, and then West to the road North of the Apple Trees.

    The wiring of the YELLOW LINE is being improved.

3. **GREEN LINE.**

    Work on improving the GREEN LINE will be commenced by the Reserve Battalions of the Brigades in the line, as soon as troops can be spared from the above for the purpose.

(c) TRAINING ARRANGEMENTS.

INFANTRY. Training is at present entirely confined to the training of specialists, such as grenadiers, Lewis gunners, Machine gunners, signallers, wiring parties, revetting parties, gas personnel &c.

This is due to the large number of working parties required to be found normally from the Reserve Brigade. These parties amount to 935 (482 required by Corps, and the remainder by the Division) for work West of the MAILLY-ENGLEBELMER line, and 640 who are employed daily east of this line in digging trenches for Signal cables.

It would be a great advantage, if a Battalion of untrained conscripts, consisting of men of more advanced years, who are not suitable for the firing line, could be attached to each Division in order to furnish working parties only, and thus permit of the Infantry when in Reserve, being trained.

At present any training, beyond that mentioned above, is practically impossible, as by the time all the specialists and working parties have been detailed, no men are left over for Company or Battalion training.

It is anticipated that the trenches for Signal cables will be completed by the 28th. This will set free some more troops for training. It is also hoped that later on, when our offensive and defensive preparations are more advanced, it will be possible to hold the line with 5 Battalions, and release the remainder for training.

TRAINING OF OFFICERS. As battalions are not utilising all their Officers with working parties, arrangements have been made to train them, by means of Battalion Exercises, carried out on the miniature enemy trenches (Scale 1 - 20) in ACHEUX Chateau grounds. Copy of the scheme and the system of working it is attached.

26 young Officers of the Division are normally undergoing instruction at the Fourth Army School and the Divisional School. (13 for 1 month at FLIXECOURT, and 13 for 3 weeks at ACHEUX).

ARTILLERY. The R.A. are fully employed on making gun emplacements, and cannot spare men for driving drill. The personnel of the Batteries recently allotted to the Division are being attached to the batteries in action, in order to obtain practical experience.

ENGINEERS. The R.E. are too fully employed on work to admit of their detailing parties for training.

VIII Corps
G. 1030.

4th Division.	B.G., "A".
29th Division.	G.O.C., R.A.
31st Division.	C.E.
48th Division.	A.P.M.
No.15 Squadron R.F.C.	A.D.A.S.

At a conference held at Corps Headquarters on May 23rd, the Corps Commander made the following remarks :

A. <u>DEFENSIVE</u>.

While our attention is directed upon the coming offensive operations, it must not be forgotten that we have an active enemy before us, and therefore must not neglect our defensive measures. The best way for the Germans to defeat our plans is to attack us before we are ready, and we must be fully prepared for this all along the line.

Points which require immediate attention are :-
The formation of -

(1) A continuous front,

(2) Support Line,

(3) A line to cover Artillery,

(4) Lateral communication between Divisions North and South, i.e., the line from FORT SUSSEX to RED COTTAGE and the opening up of PYLON AVENUE.

(5) Completion of strong points in the Yellow and Green Lines.

(6) Construction of deep dug-outs in the Support Line (we have far too many casualties at present owing to want of deep dug-outs).

(7) Fire-stepping and wiring of all communication trenches to make pockets.

(8) Construction of concrete machine gun emplacements in the Green and Yellow Lines.

It is unnecessary to have large parties of men employed on the construction of deep dug-outs and machine gun emplacements. Small permanent parties should at once be put on to the work.

B. <u>OFFENSIVE</u>.

B. OFFENSIVE.

    (1) The Commander-in-Chief has decided that the SERRE - GRANDCOURT Spur and POZIERES are to be the objectives to be attained during the first day's operations by the Left of Fourth Army.

    (2) A simultaneous attack on the GOMMECOURT Salient will be carried out by the Third Army.

    (3) The Artillery bombardment will be of the nature of a methodical bombardment and be continued until the obstacles to our advance have been adequately destroyed.

    Simultaneous wire-cutting on the Fronts of the First, Second and Third Armies will be arranged for.

2. The Commander-in-Chief desires to impress the urgent necessity for the closest supervision of the training of all troops detailed to take part in the attack. The degree of success obtainable will depend very much on the thoroughness of previous training and instruction, as well as on the completeness of the preparations made to ensure efficient co-operation and readiness to meet adequately every emergency that may arise.

3. The main idea is to gain possession of the above-mentioned line on the first day, and, having gained possession of it, for the VIII Corps and the Corps on its Right to establish a defensive flank and keep the enemy fully employed towards the North and North-East.

4. The date of the commencement of the operations has not yet been decided, and will be dependent largely upon the rapidity and efficiency of the training of the various units.

    There is no reason at present to anticipate that, on account of operations in other theatres of war, we may be asked

(3)

asked to engage upon our task prematurely. The danger of that has apparently passed.

We have been promised at least three weeks notice before the date is finally fixed.

5. As regards the bombardment, looking at the operations as a whole, we shall have twice as many guns for the bombardment as we had at LOOS, and we shall have practically an unlimited supply of ammunition, dependent, of course, to a certain extent upon the date.

The bombardment will be a deliberate undertaking, and we want to make full use of all the various engines of war that we now have at our disposal.

6. We are to attack on a front rather more than twice as wide as we attacked on at LOOS, we have a great many more reserves at our disposal than we had then, and, moreover, a simultaneous attack will be carried out by the French on our Right on a considerably wider front than ours.

The distance of our objective from our Front Line is practically the same as that gained by us at LOOS.

7. It is of the highest importance that there should be the closest touch and co-operation between ourselves and the French, and also between each Corps and Division of our Army. Corps and Divisions can assist one another very much by maintaining touch, and by placing guns for enfilading their respective fronts in the areas of the Corps or Division on their right and left. When the VIII Corps has gained some ground, its batteries can greatly assist the X Corps by pushing forward to enfilade the enemy's second line in front of the X Corps. The same thing can be done by the X Corps in order to assist the VIII Corps.

8. As regards the working out of Artillery Time Tables we have almost always on former occasions been too quick and not allowed enough time for the Artillery to really cover

<u>the advance</u>

the advance of the Infantry. If we can get our Infantry forward to the GRANDCOURT Ridge in three hours from the moment of the assault we shall have done very well indeed.

9. A point in connection with the Artillery which must not be lost sight of, is the very heavy work that is thrown on gun detachments during a sustained bombardment which will be carried on day and night. We have asked for an addition to establishment of 40 men per battery of Field Artillery, but it is probable that only 20 of these will be available.

10. The wire-cutting problem is not an easy one. In some cases, the more distant wire can be cut by 60 prs, but it is very difficult to tell whether it has been effectively cut. Aeroplane observation, in combination with observation from the ground, helps.

11. 18 prs concealed in emplacements close up to the front trenches and not used till the moment of the assault, have in the past proved very useful, and are to be arranged for both to assist the assault and to cut the distant wire.

12. In considering the operations as a whole, we must never forget that "the hardest part of the nut is the shell", and if we do not get through the front trench, our preparations for the attack on the enemy's back lines will be useless.

13. As regards training, there has been some difficulty about getting ground. We have got the BUS-LOUVENCOURT ground for the 29th and 31st Divisions. We have the use of the ST.RIQUIER ground for the 4th Division, and we hope shortly to have a bit of ground S.W. of DOULLENS for the 48th Division.

We want to train particularly for the assault which we have before us, over the same distances, out of trenches, and against and over trenches of the same trace as those each Brigade will have to push over.

<u>Infantry</u>

(5).

~~Infantry must lay~~ out on their training grounds ~~facsimile~~ of the German trenches they are going to attack and facsimile of our trenches from which the attack is going to be made.

Some at least of this, say a Company front, should be actually dug.

In digging trenches for practice purposes arrangements must be made to disguise them so as to prevent them being seen by enemy aeroplanes.

14. The passing of one body of troops through another to the attack of more distant objectives is not an easy operation, and should be constantly practised by Brigades which will have to undertake it.

15. The question of water is going to be a very important one, and too much stress cannot be laid on the training of men to be economical with the water in their water bottles. The question of water will have a good deal to say to our success or failure to maintain ourselves in our new positions.

16. <u>MACHINE GUNS AND STOKES MORTARS.</u>

The tactical training of machine gun batteries, Lewis gunners and Stokes Mortar Batteries must be taken in hand at once. Batteries of these should work with battalions and Brigades whenever they are practising an attack on enemy's trenches

It must be impressed on machine gunners that they must use every effort to get well forward, even moving in the front line of attack. The tendency at present is for machine gunners to remain too far behind.

There must be a certain number of Stokes Mortars told off to move forward with the Infantry during the assault, to be ready to take on any strong points which may hold up the infantry.

17. Divisions will consider the formations infantry should adopt when making the assault. Should a company for instance - assault on a front of one platoon or a front of two platoons. Should platoons move in line extended or in columns of extended sections.

The troops detailed to assault the first line system of trenches should move in lines (waves), each wave moving up through communication trenches to our front trench and assault from there. As soon as the enemy's front line has been capture the remaining troops told off to assault the second and third objectives will move overland in small columns until owing to the intensity of the enemy's fire it becomes necessary to exten into line.

18. Stress is laid on the importance of assaulting troops starting on a line parallel with the front to be assaluted. In order to ensure this it may be necessary to put out the night before a line of pickets or a tape to show the line on which each wave should form up before moving on to the assault.

In moving forward overland the route must be carefully reconnoitred so as to make sure that existing wire on our back lines does not interfere with the movement, and bridges for crossing trenches must be prepared.

19. COMMUNICATION.

It is impossible to have too many alternative measures for passing information. Visual signalling, telephones, runners, flares, electric lamps must all be made use of, and carefully practised from now onwards.

The importance of having a supply of well trained orderlies cannot be overrated, men who know their way about al the trenches on the Divisional front, know the positions of Company, Battalion and Brigade Headquarters, position of dumps waterpipes and place where water bottles can be filled, etc.

Signalling

Signalling between aeroplanes and infantry is now being practised but the results have not been very satisfactory. It is hoped that matters will improve with further practice and experience.

20. The marking out of roads across our trenches and the preparation of bridges to carry the roads both over our and the enemy's trenches must be taken in hand at once. The roads allotted to each Division were laid down in my G. 511 dated 23/4/16.

In several places trenches now run under existing roads. These points must be examined and made strong enough to bear the weight of motor transport.

The question of "sign-posting" trenches must receive very careful attention. There must be a sign-post at every junction of trenches.

Not only must sign-posts be erected in all trenches, at crossing places and turnings but careful arrangements must be made to post police or sentries to render it impossible for men to move the reverse way in "up" and "down" trenches. It is not sufficient to place a sentry at the commencement of an "up" or "down" trench, but sentries must be posted at any points where lateral trenches run into these "up" and "down" trenches.

Arrangements must be made to post police in the communication trenches to regulate the flow of traffic and to deal with "skulkers".

21. IDENTIFICATION MARKS.

Divisions must carefully preserve and collect all tin cases in order to make the 9" triangular tin identification marks to put on the mens backs. Arrangements are being made to manufacture the coloured collapsible screens to be carried by platoons and companies.

22.

22. **CARRYING OF PACKS.**

This question to be discussed. If it is decided that packs should not be carried, arrangements to be made for their storage. What should be left in the packs? What besides the iron ration should be carried in the haversack?

23. **PROVOST MARSHALS AND BATTLE POLICE.**

Brigade Posts will be placed in communication trenches about 500 yards in rear of front line to deal with any sudden panic.

Divisional Posts will be placed, generally speaking, along the line ENGLEBELMER - MAILLY MAILLET - AUCHONVILLERS - COLINCAMPS - SAILLY AU BOIS. When stopped by Divisional posts the men will be collected, marched to the Divisional Stragglers posts, which are in the vicinity of dressing stations. At the stragglers posts they will be fed and if necessary re-armed and eventually marched back in the evening to their units as a formed body.

The A.P.M. of a Division should be in immediate charge of the Divisional Posts. It should be exceptional for him to go forward to the Brigade line.

24. Working parties should commence work earlier during hot weather.

25. **REINFORCEMENTS.**

About 10% of the men and all officers surplus to 3 per company to be left behind to form reinforcements to come up after the first day of battle.

Reinforcements (Officers and men) to be left at the dumps.

H.Q., VIII Corps.
23rd May, 1916.

W. Ruthven
B.G., G.S.
VIII Corps.

SECRET.

Appendix 10

29th DIVISIONAL CONFERENCE NO. 9
Held on
23rd May 1916.

RAIDS.	1. The G.O.C. requested Brigadiers to consider their action in the event of a heavy bombardment or of a raid. He suggested that communication trenches should be barred with iron doors and the portion of trench in front of the iron door covered with wire netting to prevent the enemy throwing bombs over the door into our portion of the trench, both sides of the communication trench to be protected by wire entanglements. They should also consider the question of the cooperation of machine guns, Lewis guns and trench mortars in this connection.
POSITION OF F.O.Os.	2. It was decided that the F.O.O. should remain during the night at Battalion Headquarters, as is done at present. Detailed instructions for the F.O.O. will be issued.
TESTS FOR ARTILLERY SUPPORT.	3. The time taken for artillery to bring fire on to the enemy's trenches should be tested by Brigades at least once in every two days, and the result of the test reported to these Headquarters. The time should be taken from the moment that the F.O.O. is requested to give support. In order to avoid discrepancies, the officer making the test should compare his watch with that of the F.O.O.
BATTALION AREAS.	4. The Battalions in the front line should be given a fixed area for maintenance, sanitation, etc. This area should stretch from the front line back to the reserve trenches.
MACHINE GUNS.	5. Arrangements should as far as possible be made to connect machine guns by telephone to the Battalion Headquarters on the front over which the guns fire.
TRENCH MORTARS.	6. The Medium and Light Trench Mortars, situated in the areas held by Battalions, will be at the disposal of the Battalion Commanders for retaliation, etc. Battalion Commanders should get into touch with the officers commanding these mortar batteries and arrange for their cooperation when required. Light trench mortars should not be stationed in the front trenches, but should be kept in the support trenches, in positions which will enable them to bring fire to bear on our own front line, so as to be able to drive the enemy out of our line should they succeed in temporarily occupying it.
FRONT LINE GARRISON.	7. The front line will only be occupied by the troops allotted to it as garrison. In some places, the front line is now being held unnecessarily strongly. Posts of 1 N.C.O. and 3 men by day, and 1 N.C.O. and 6 men by night, at intervals along the front line, are under present conditions sufficient. Troops in the front line are strictly prohibited to utilize it for purposes of eating, sleeping or washing.

(2).

ATTACHMENT OF INFANTRY OFFICERS TO ARTILLERY. 8. It has been decided for the present not to attach senior infantry officers to artillery units for training. There is however no objection to the attachment of junior infantry officers, if they can be spared.

REDUCTION OF TROOPS HOLDING FRONT LINE. 9. The G.O.C. decided that it was not feasible at present to hold the front line system with three Battalions and two Battalions in reserve, at MAILLY-MAILLET and ENGEEBELMER respectively. This system has been tried and found not to answer.

MARCH DISCIPLINE. 11. Attention should be paid to the march discipline of small detachments of R.A., Infantry, and A.S.C., which has not yet come up to standard. Smartness in trenches and in billets must be insisted on; there is still considerable room for improvement in the matter of saluting.

TRAINING OF YOUNG OFFICERS. 12. Young officers require to be taught before they can be expected to train their men. They should therefore be given instruction by senior officers in the correct method of carrying out attacks, etc., so that they may possess the necessary knowledge for teaching others, and acquire that confidence in dealing with their men, which can only be obtained from the feeling that they possess more knowledge.

BATTALION EXERCISES. 13. The facsimile of the trenches in Acheux Chateau grounds will be found an excellent means of imparting instruction. Two Battalion exercises for use with this ground have been issued. The hostile trenches will be marked out full size on the new training ground near LOUVENCOURT, and Battalions can then be exercised over it in the attack, etc.

WORKING PARTIES. 14. Work should commence early, 5 or 6.0 am., so that work during the heat of the day can be avoided.

BATHS. 15. Attention was called to the fact that the Division is not using the baths at ACHEUX and MAILLY-MAILLET to their full extent.

CORPS CONFERENCE. 16. The G.O.C. drew attention to the various points regarding defensive and offensive action, which had been brought to notice by Corps Commander on the morning of the 23rd. A copy of the minutes of the Corps Conference, G 1030, is attached. Special attention is directed to paragraph 15 (Offensive) of the Conference, regarding the necessity for training troops to be economical in the use of water. Men should be trained not to drink until the evening.

C.F. Fuller

24th May 1916.

Lieut.Colonel, G.S.
29th Division.

appendix 11

SECRET.   COPY No. 11.

Reference
Map 1/40,000.

31st DIVISION ORDER No 19.

22.5.16.

1. The 88th Bde Machine Gun Company will be relieved in the front line on the 23rd instant by the 92nd and 94th Bde Machine Gun Companies.

   The 92nd Bde Machine Gun Company will take over the emplacements in the 93rd Inf. Bde Sector and the 94th Bde Machine Gun Company those in the 94th Inf. Bde Sector.

2. Details regarding the relief will be arranged between the Brigade Commanders concerned.

3. The 88th Bde Machine Gun Company will move when relieved to ENGLEBELMER coming under the orders of G.O.C. 29th Division on arrival.

               H.W. Stenhouse major
               for Lieut-Colonel.,
                   General Staff.
                   31st Division.

Issued at   11-30. a.m.

92 Inf.Bde.	Copy No	1.
93 Inf.Bde.	" "	2.
94 Inf.Bde.	" "	3.
31 Divl.Signals.	" "	4.
"A" Branch.	" "	5.
A.P.M.	" "	6.
31 Divl.Train.	" "	7.
S.S.O. 31 Div.	" "	8.
A.D.M.S.	" "	9.
A.D.V.S.	" "	10.
29th Div.	" "	11.
(for information)		
Office Copy.	" "	12.
War Diary.	" "	13.

Appendix 12 War Diary

NOTES FOR CORPS CONFERENCE AT 10.0 am.
on 26th May 1916.

(a). A full size facsimile of the German trenches is being traced on the training ground. It is intended to exercise Battalions and Brigades in attack practices.

(b). It is proposed to plough the trench lines, so that they should be invisible from an aeroplane. A photograph will be taken to ensure that this is the case.

(c). A miniature facsimile of the German trenches and of our own front line on a scale of 1/20 has been spitlocked in Acheux Chateau grounds. All officers and N.C.Os. attending the Divisional School, and the officers of the Brigade in reserve, are exercised in schemes on this ground, which include arrangements for selecting and consolidating strong points in the hostile trenches. Copies of schemes are attached.

(i). It is hoped to do this later, but the difficulty of getting sufficient men together owing to the great drain on them for working parties, makes training at present impossible, vide statement of employment of Reserve Brigade attached.

(ii). Yes. It is proposed that 30 men of each consolidating platoon should carry 25 sandbags and a pick or shovel per man. The balance should form a special wiring party (about 12 men) and would carry rolls of barbed wire, wire cutters, hedging gloves and stakes.

(iii). Yes. Practice has been carried out in the bombing grounds, but only by squads, made up mostly of N.C.Os. (vide (i))

(d). This is still under discussion – probably line of platoon columns i.e each platoon in column of sections for first system. The advance against the 2nd and 3rd objectives in columns of half platoons in fours or files extending at close ranges.

(2).

(e). One young officer and 4 N.C.Os. from each Battalion are given a three weeks course and are trained in accordance with the attached syllabus. It is proposed to train 2 officers and 3 N.C.Os per Battalion in future.

(f). Nil. Officers are trained under Battalion arrangements.

(g). Each Battery has a certain number of reinforcements trained, and are training more whenever their Brigade is in reserve. The Batteries belonging to Brigades in the front line are fully employed in constructing gun emplacements and have no opportunity for training extra personnel.

(h). Syllabus of instruction for classes under Divisional Grenadier Officer, and for Battalion Grenadiers are attached. The total number of grenadiers trained is attached. Battalions have classes of 32 men in training at a time, when the Brigade is in reserve.

(i). The C.R.A. has arranged to have one 2" T.M. Battery at a time trained on the new training ground under the Divisional T.M. Officer - 3 officers and 21 other ranks are already trained as reinforcements.

(j). Battalions are training their existing signallers. when in reserve. and also the additional men, whose training was commenced at SUEZ. It takes a long time, however, for the ordinary soldier to be turned into a trained signaller. 25 men are doing refresher courses under Corps arrangements.

Appendix 13

SECRET.

Copy No. 3

29th DIVISION ORDER NO. 33.

Reference: 57 D. Map 1/10,000.   26th May, 1916.

1.   The 87th Brigade will relieve the 88th Brigade in the Right Sector of the Line on the night of the 28/29th May, and will report to these Headquarters when the relief is completed.

2.   The 88th Brigade on relief from the Right Sector on the night of 28/29th inst. will relieve the 86th Brigade in the Left Sector and will report to these Headquarters when the relief is completed. The 86th Brigade on relief will be billeted at LOUVENCOURT, and will be in Corps Reserve.

3.   The Brigade Machine Gun Companies will move with their respective Brigades.

4.   Brigades will report their respective dispositions to these Headquarters by 12.Noon on the 29th inst.

5.   The reliefs may be carried out during daylight, provided that the troops are marched to and from the forward area in small parties.

G. Fuller.
Lieut. Colonel, G.S.
29th Division

Issued at 5.45 p.m.

Copy No. 1-3 General Staff.
      4 86th Brigade.
      5 87th Brigade.
      6 88th Brigade.
      7-11 Headquarters, R.A.
      12 C.R.E.
      13 Officer i/c Signals.
      14 A.A. & Q.M.G.
      15 A.P.M.
      16 O.C. Divisional Train.
      17 A.D.V.S.
      18 A.D.M.S.
      19 D.A.D.O.S.
      20 VIII Corps.   )
      21 31st Division.) for
      22 36th Division.) information.

87th Bde

For your information
& return, pse.

C. Fuller
29/5/16   Lt Col.

To 29th Divn –
Herewith 26th Divn
orders returned –

/s Shirley Cookson
Capt.
for A/Bde Major

[illegible signature]
30/5/16

HEADQUARTERS
No. 1109
Date 31/5/16
87th INFANTRY BRIGADE

SECRET

Appendix 14

36th DIVISION ORDER NO. 27

Copy No. 4

28th May 1916

1. The following re-distribution of Brigades will take place on the 30th and 31st instant:-

   The 107th Brigade will relieve the 108th Brigade in the line
   The 108th Brigade will move into the training area
   The 109th Brigade will relieve the 107th Brigade in the MARTINSART-HEDAUVILLE area for providing working parties.

2. The necessary moves consequent on this re-distribution are shown in attached table.

3. The G.O.C., 107th Brigade will take over Command of the front line when the relief of the battalions in the trenches is completed.

4. The 109th Brigade will take over the Headquarters of the 108th Brigade at 12 noon on 31st instant. Battalions of the 109th Brigade will be under the orders of the G.O.C., 107th Brigade until the arrival of the Headquarters of the 109th Brigade.

5. The 109th Brigade Machine Gun Company will furnish the 8 Vickers Guns in the THIEPVAL WOOD Sub-sector, relieving the 107th Brigade Machine Gun Company which will take over the HAMEL Sub-sector.

6. Details of reliefs of units in the line will be arranged between Brigades, but no movements of troops in larger formation than companies at 4 minutes interval will take place during daylight East of a line through HEDAUVILLE - FORCEVILLE.

7. X 36 Trench Mortar Battery will take over duties with the Trench Mortars in action, relieving Y 36 Battery which will take over working party duties in THIEPVAL WOOD. Z 36 Battery will continue working in THIEPVAL WOOD. The Stoke's Batteries will remain at VARENNES for training.

8. **Transport.** Transport of the 107th Brigade will remain as at present.
   Transport of the 108th and 109th Brigades will interchange - Arrangements to be made direct between Brigades concerned.

9. During the progress of the relief working parties available for work under the C. R. E. will be as follows:-

   30th (Day) and Night of 30/31st
       8th R. Ir. Rif. and ½ Battn 9th R. Innis. Fus.
   31st (Day)
       9th R. Innis. Fus.   11th R. Innis. Fus.
   31st /1st (Night of)
       9th R. Innis. Fus., 11th R. Innis. Fus., & 14th R. Ir. Rif.
   1st and subsequently
       Whole of 109th Brigade.

P. T. O.

- 2 -

10. Completion of reliefs will be reported to Divisional Headquarters.

Issued at 6/30 p.m.

LT. COLONEL.
G.S.

Copies to:-

1. G.O.C.
2/3. Xth Corps.
4. 89th Division
5. 32nd Division
6. 49th Division
7. "Q" Branch
8. C. R. A.
9. C. R. E.
10. 6th Innis. Dns.
11. 36th Cyclist Coy
12. 107th Brigade.
13. 108th Brigade.
14. 109th Brigade.
15. 16th R. Ir. Rif (P)
16. 36th Div. Train
17. 36th Div. Supply Col.
18. A. D. M. S
19. 36th Signal Coy.
20. File
21. War Diary.

TABLE OF RELIEFS

DATE	BRIGADE	UNIT	FROM	TO	TIME	RELIEVING	WHO MOVE TO
30th	109th	9th R.Innis.Fus ½ Battn	FORCEVILLE	HEDAUVILLE	arrive 12 noon	15th R.Ir.Rif. ½ Battn	MESNIL & MOUND KEEP.
30th	107th	15th R.Ir.Rif	FORCEVILLE & HEDAUVILLE	MESNIL & MOUND KEEP	arrive 1.pm MOUND KEEP relief to be carried out by inter-Battalion arrangements	9th R.Ir.Fus.	VARENNES
30th	109th	11th R.Innis. Fus.	VARENNES	MARTINSART WOOD	Arrive 6.p.m.	9th R.Ir.Rif.	THIEPVAL Sub-Sector
30th	109th	14th R.Ir.Rif.	LEALVILLERS	MESNIL MARTINSART	Leave LEALVILLERS 7.p.m.	10th R.Ir.Rif.	HAMEL Sub-sector
30th	108th	9th R.Ir.Fus.	MESNIL & MOUND KEEP	VARENNES	Leave MESNIL 11am	11th R.Innis. Fus.	MARTINSART WOOD
30th	107th	9th R.Ir.Rif	MARTINSART WOOD	THIEPVAL Sub-sector	as arranged by 107th & 108th Brigades.	13th R.Ir.Rif.	LEALVILLERS
30th	108th	13th R.Ir.Rif.	THIEPVAL Trenches	LEALVILLERS		14th R.Ir.Rif. (leave at 7.p.m. 30th)	MARTINSART & MESNIL
Night 30/31st	107th	10th R.Ir.Rif.	MARTINSART & MESNIL	HAMEL Sub-sector		12 R.Ir.Rif	FORCEVILLE
Night 30/31st	108th	12 R.Ir.Rif.	HAMEL Trenches	FORCEVILLE		9 R.Innis.Fus (½ Battn) & 15 R.Ir.Rif. (½ Battn)	HEDAUVILLE

- 2 -

DATE	BRIGADE	UNIT	FROM	TO	TIME	RELIEVING	WHO MOVE TO
31st	109th	10 R.Innis. Fus.	LEALVILLERS	MARTINSART WOOD	arrive 12 noon	8 R.Ir.Rif.	THIEPVAL & MARTINSART
31st	107th	8th R.Ir.Rif.	MARTINSART WOOD	THIEPVAL (MARTINSART)	arrive 10 a.m.	11 R.I. Rif.	LEALVILLERS
31st	108th	11 R.Ir.Rif.	THIEPVAL & MARTINSART	LEALVILLERS	Leave on relief by 8 R.Ir Rif	10. R. Innis. Fus.	MARTINSART WOOD
31st	109th	BDE. H.Q.	HARPONVILLE	MARTINSART		108th Bde.H.Q.	HARPONVILLE
31st	109th	BDE. M.G. Coy.	VARENNES	MARTINSART (8 guns to THIEPVAL WOOD Sub-Sector.	Night of 31st	107 Bde. M.G. Coy.	MARTINSART
31st	107th	BDE. M.G. Coy.	MARTINSART & THIEPVAL WOOD Sub-Sector	MARTINSART (8 guns to HAMEL Sub-sector)	as arranged by 107 and 108 Brigades.	108th Brigade.	HARPONVILLE
31st	108th	Brigade H.Q.	MARTINSART	HARPONVILLE		109th Bde. H.Q.	MARTINSART

S E C R E T   Copy No. 4

36th DIVISION ORDER NO. 28.

29th May 1916.

1. The 107th Brigade will relieve the 108th Brigade in the line to-morrow as follows:-

UNIT.	FROM	TO	RELIEVING
9th R.Ir.Rif.	MARTINSART WOOD	THIEPVAL Sub-sector	13th R. Ir. Rif.
10th R.Ir.Rif.	MARTINSART & MESNIL	HAMEL Sub-Sector.	12th R. Ir. Rif.
8th R.Ir.Rif.	MARTINSART WOOD	THIEPVAL & MARTINSART	11th R. Ir. Rif.
15th R. Ir.Rif.	WILL NOT MOVE		

2. The Battalions of the 108th Brigade will move into the billets vacated by the battalions of the 107th Brigade who relieve them.

3. Details of the reliefs will be arranged between the two Brigades.

4. The G.O.C., 107th Brigade, will take over the Command of the front line when the relief of the Battalions in the trenches is completed.

5. The Machine Gun Companies of the 107th and 108th Brigades will retain their present positions.

6. Completion of reliefs will be reported to Divisional Headquarters

Issued at 6/45 pm.   W. B. Spender

Copies to:-   CAPTAIN G.S.

    1. G.O.C.
    2/3. Xth Corps.
    4. 29th Division
    5. 32nd Division
    6. 49th Division   15. 36th Div. Supply Col.
    7. "Q" Branch   16. A. D. M. S.
    8. C. R. A.   17. 36th Signal Coy.
    9. C. R. E.   18. File
    10. 107th Brigade.   19. War Diary.
    11. 108th Brigade.
    12. 109th Brigade.
    13. 16th R. Ir. Rif (P)
    14. 36th Div. Train.

29TH DIVISION DAILY SUMMARY.
for
Period 6 a.m. 30/4/16 to 6 a.m. 1/5/16.

OPERATIONS.

ARTILLERY.

Our guns at intervals throughout the day fired on the trenches in front of, N. of, and behind BEAUMONT HAMEL. So far as our sector was concerned, the enemy's only response was at 4.15.p.m. to fire six rounds shrapnel at a working party of ours.

During the night our Artillery dispersed a working party opposite Q.10.12.

Our aeroplanes came in for heavy fire from artillery as well as from machine guns firing from the N. of BEAUMONT HAMEL.

Enemy machine guns were busy during the day firing at our aeroplanes and at night on our front line.

MINENWERFER.

Fired 6 times at the salient MARY REDAN during the night. Two were "duds". Our Artillery fire reply was late and did not appear to do any damage.

Three more rounds were fired near salient this morning. Two of the bombs fell in the vicinity of NEW TRENCH and were judged to come from communication trenches at about 1514 in Q.17a 99-09.

PATROLS.

Our covering party in front of Q.10-6 reported German Patrol of 4 men who came up near our wire at this point about 8 p.m.

INTELLIGENCE.

ENEMY WORK.

Parties carrying timber:- between 5 p.m. and 5.30 p.m. One party was about 40 strong.:- supposed pit props, a sack of what looked like meal, a few picks and shovels, were observed in BEAUMONT HAMEL.

Work proceeding especially about Q.11c5.5 where it looks as if a big communication trench is being made.

Work is going on steadily in front of MARY REDAN. Enemy heard repairing wire at this point during the night. Lewis gun was turned on them and shrapnel burst right amongst them at 12.0 a.m.

Clay was seen being thrown up at Q.d.65-82 and wiring was going on near there during the night.

ENEMY MOVEMENT.

About 3.30 p.m. a few small parties each consisting of from 4 to 5 men in full marching order passed through the village -- possible reinforcements.

TRAINS AND TRANSPORT.

Train activity normal.

At 8.30 a.m. two wagons observed on STATION ROAD going NORTH. At about 10.30 a.m. transport wagons seen at same place travelling in same direction.

WIRE.

Our wire has suffered a little from the bombardment of 29/30 April; enemy wire has been considerably damaged (1) from HAWTHORN REDOUBT to within 60 yards of the SUNK ROAD. (2) from this point to the road, the wire has been repaired with wooden stakes. (3) from the road northwards for 200 yards the wire has been badly cut up and little has been done to repair it. (4) wire north of BEAUMONT HAMEL seems to be intact.

MISCELLANEOUS.

- 2 -

MISCELLANEOUS.

SIGNALS.

On the evening of the raid, light signalling was noticed taking place at ENGLEBELMER about 7.45 to 8.15 p.m. (Reported by 87th Brigade M.G.O.)

1/5/16.

Captain,
G.S., 29th Division.

29TH DIVISION DAILY SUMMARY.
for
Period from 6 a.m. 1/5/16 to 6 a.m. 2/5/16.

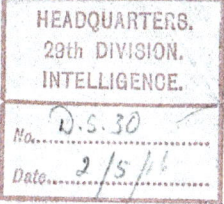

HEADQUARTERS.
29th DIVISION.
INTELLIGENCE.

No. D.S.30
Date. 2/5/16

OPERATIONS.

ARTILLERY.
At 4 a.m. 6 H.E. shells destroyed some of F.O.O's wire without doing further damage.

ENEMY RAID.
At about 8.30 p.m. a party of the enemy suddenly rushed up to our wire on the right of No. 2 sap at Q.17-15 and threw 12 bombs into our wire. Our men immediately stood to and fired on the party who ran away. Hostile Artillery then opened up a violent bombardment with H.E. Shrapnel and Minenwerfer bombs, the latter fired in salvoes of three. This lasted about 15 to 20 minutes when the fire was raised. Our men immediately manned the fire step and by flares could see a party of the enemy between 30 and 50 yards outside the enemy's barbed wire. Heavy rifle and Lewis gun fire was opened on them. The enemy broke and ran off.
Shapp sniping was then carried on for about an hour when things quieted down for the rest of the night.
A patrol was sent out to try and bring in any Germans left out but none could be found.

MACHINE GUN.
A machine Gun emplacement or observation post has been erected at Q.6.c.7/89. (By cyclists).

INTELLIGENCE.

ENEMY MOVEMENTS.
(a) The following were observed from Q.4.7.
(1) 8 men carrying boxes which might have contained bombs
(2) 12 men carrying 6 poles which seemed to be 12' long.
(3) 30 men carrying boards 3' by 1' marchingxorder
(4) At 9.15 a.m. an officer and 12 men in full marching order passing southward through BEAUMONT HAMEL.
(5) At 4.15 p.m. an office and 10 men in greyish uniform with caps without peaks carrying a roll of barbed wire. The Officers wore a bluish uniform with burnished shoulder chains and black boots reaching to the knees.
(6) At 5.15 p.m. 2 officers in dark grey uniforms, black boots reaching to the knees and peak caps. One of them had a red diamond - shaped patch in front of his cap.

TRAINS AND TRANSPORT.
(b) (1) At 10 p.m. what might have been a traction engine at work at BEAUMONT HAMEL was heard. The right sub-sector report a train moving from North to South from B.H. at 3.30 and heavy transport wagons close to B.H. at 3.45 a.m.
(2) About eight 2 horse wagons were seen on RAILWAY ROAD going North.

(c) ENEMY WORK.
(1) At 9 a.m. metallic sounds indicated that girders or iron plates were being moved in BEAUMONT HAMEL. At 3.30 p.m. a working party was seen throwing up earth from the trench in the wood in front of Q.4.7. (Both reported by Infantry)
(2) New work reported in front line trenches nearly opposite Q.17-22. Fresh earth thrown up.

MISCELLANEOUS.

AEROPLANES.
During the whole of the day at least one aeroplane was up. At 9-10 and 9-25 a.m. one was observed to bank and fire with his machine gun on to the enemy's trenches opposite to Q.4.8. The principal M.G. Fire in response came from three positions in HAWTHORN REDOUBT.

PIGEONS./

- 2 -

PIGEONS.
2 Pigeons were observed to fly from behind our lines to enemy lines and settle on a hay-rick opposite Q.10.8. (Reported by Infantry).

FLARES.
At 8.15 p.m. 2 red flares were followed by 2 Shrapnel shells and a burst of M.G. fire. At 8.40 p.m. MINENWERFER bombardment which appeared to be directed outside both flanks of our sector, was immediately preceded by the ascent of two parachute flares. At 9.15 4 four more went simultaneously and the bombardment ceased. (Reported by Infantry). During the bombardment several red and several white flares were sent up.

SIGNALS.
Following lights were seen before shelling began 3 red rockets in a group. Towards the end; white, green, white.

SHELLS.
Shells have fallen in this area which have a double explosion with an interval of about a second between each explosion.

W. M. Armstrong.

2nd May, 1916.

Captain,
G.S., 29th Division.

29TH DIVISIONAL DAILY SUMMARY.

for

Period from 6 a.m. 2/5/16 to 6 a.m. 3/5/16.

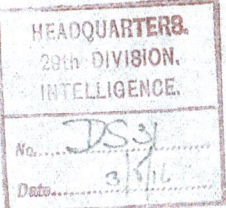

OPERATIONS.

ARTILLERY.

Our Artillery was more active than that of the enemy; shelling different parts of the line at intervals during the day. About 1.30 the enemy again shelled the portion of the left sub-sector between Q.4.2 and Q.4.6. and compelled a working party in ST. HELEN STREET to take cover. The night was quiet.

About 5 to 5.30 p.m. some shells got into our trench in the Right Sub-Sector enfilading from the Left. 3 men were wounded.

MACHINE GUNS.

Enemy Machine Guns were not as active as usual. Machine Gun position reported at Q.17 b 0.0.4.8.

INTELLIGENCE.

ENEMY MOVEMENTS.

From the "Peep-show" in Q.4.Z numerous fatigue parties could be observed carrying planks of various lengths, pit props, bundles of sandbags, picks and shovels, piping, corrugated iron sheets, boxes, (probably of bombs), and stores. A number of men passing backwards and forwards who wore a grey uniform and a cap with a light blue band round it. At 6.10 p.m. an officer was seen on a cycle who wore a dark grey uniform and cap with peak and red band. Two other cyclists were seen at 5 p.m. and 6 p.m. respectively. Some of the parties on fatigue were accompanied by soldiers with fixed bayonets.

ENEMY WORK.

Many flares were sent up from the enemy lines during the night. A covering party on SUNKEN ROAD reported enemy working in trenches opposite Q.16.4 apparently building parapet as sounds were heard like hammering on sandbags with shovels.

In earthworks at Q.6c.67.4 there seems to be an observation post or Machine Gun emplacement. A narrow slit in the earthworks is visible.

An observation post or Machine Gun emplacement at Q.6c.7.98 is very strong. Earth with growing grass has been placed in front, it has a flat top with a good thickness of earth on it.

TRAINS AND TRANSPORT.

The following train movements were seen:-
11.30 to ACHIET-LE-GRAND from BAPAUME
4 o'Clock   do.   do   do.
5.15   to BAPAUME from ACHIET-LE-GRAND
5.45   to ACHIET-LE-GRAND from BAPAUME
5.55   do.   do.   do.   do.

ENEMY WIRE.

Enemy has strengthened his wire considerably opposite point of REDAN N.E. to Q.17a8.9 where it is very high.

MISCELLANEOUS.

AEROPLANES.

From 6 a.m. to 9 a.m. and from 4 p.m. to Dusk our 'planes were scouting. A few shells were fired at them in the morning.

W.M. Armstrong.

3rd May, 1916.

Captain,
G.S., 29th Division.

29TH DIVISION DAILY SUMMARY

for

Period from 6 a.m. 3/5/16 to 6 a.m. 4/5/16.

HEADQUARTERS.
29th DIVISION.
INTELLIGENCE.
No. D.S. 32
Date 4/5/16

OPERATIONS.

ARTILLERY. *field artillery*
Enemy whizz-bangs fired during the day at intervals from a position which has not yet been satisfactorily located, but is N.E. of Q.16.4.

About 15 H.E. shells were fired into support trenches in the Left sub-sector during the afternoon.

At 5 a.m. 5 whizz-bangs were fired over BOND STREET.

Enemy Artillery shelled our working party in Q.4.6 and ESAU'S WAY during the forenoon. Soil thronw up by our working party is thought to have been observed by the enemy. Our O.P. at Q.4.7. was damaged, 5 shells bursting close to it.

Enemy Artillery shelled our lines at Q.10.12. about 7.45 a.m. with six 7.7 shells causing several casualties. CARDIFF STREET and SECOND AVENUE were shelled rather heavily in the morning. No damage was done to machine gun emplacements. MINDEN TRENCH and ST. HELEN'S TRENCH were shelled about 2 p.m.

MACHINE GUNS.
Machine guns on both sides were fairly active during the night on the right of the Left Sub-sector. The Machine Gun emplacements reported on 2/5/16 are located at Q.10.d.6.7 and Q.10.d.7.9. respectively.

PATROLS.
A patrol was ent out from our line at JACOB'S LADDER at 12 midnight. The following report was received from Capt. R.C. Wynter, 4th Worcester Regiment, who was in charge of the patrol.

"At midnight on 3/4th May a patrol of 2 Officers, 1 Sergeant, and 9 Other ranks left our trenches from JACOB'S LADDER. It was intended to reconnoitre the SUNKEN ROAD just North of NEW BEAUMONT ROAD. The patrol got within 10 yards of the SUNKEN ROAD when without any warning rifle fire was opened from the other side of the road. (Q.4.d.45.35). The patrol lay down immediately, but the rifle fire was maintained by the enemy and almost instantaneously a bomb was thrown followed by 2 more bombs and more rifle fire. The distance of our patrol from the enemy was not more than 20 yards. In my opinion and from what I could judge this party of the enemy is a permanent detached post. I consider that this position is entrnched and a communication runs back to the hostile trench. The strength of this hostile post was in my opinion approximately 6, riflemen and 2 bombers."

INTELLIGENCE.

ENEMY MOVEMENTS.
The sound of wood and rails being unloaded in BEAUMONT HAMEL was heard during the night. A party working in the open at about Q.11.c.54. was dispersed by our snipers.

Between dawn and 10.10 a.m. 65 men were counted going along the road in BEAUMONT HAMEL, 2 were armed, 49 were unarmed and 14 carrying loads. Corrugated Iron and mining props were being carried.

ENEMY WORK.
Enemy heard wiring in front of ROONEY'S SAP. A Field Gun located at Q.5.d.25.50. Our artillery silenced the gun with H.E.

SNIPERS.
Active on enemy's side.

MISCELLANEOUS.

SIGNALS.

SIGNALS.
On the evening of the 2nd between 9 and 9.30 signalling was observed in the enemy's front line, about point Q.11.c.00.33. It seemed to be signalling towards ENGLEBELMER, bot no answering flashes were seen. The flash resembled that of an ordinary signalling lamp in colour and size and a dot dash code was being used.

PIGEONS.
Two pigeons reported on 2/5/16 were seen about 6 a.m. on the 1st inst.. They were bluish in colour. Later in the day a sentry in Q.44 reported a Pigeon flying fom the direction of BEAUMONT HAMEL towards AUCHONVILLERS at 5.20 p.m.; at 6 p.m. he saw another flying in the opposite direction.

FLARES.
Flares were sent up frequently during the night by the enemy.

4/5/16.

Captain,
G.S., 29th Division.

29TH DIVISION DAILY SUMMARY.
for
Period from 6 a.m. 4/5/16 to 6 a.m. 5/5/16

HEADQUARTERS,
29th DIVISION,
INTELLIGENCE.

No. DS 32a
Date 5/5/16

OPERATIONS.
ARTILLERY.
The period was on the whole quiet. At 9 a.m. the enemy bombarded the new part of 1st AVENUE with about a dozen shells. At 8.30 p.m. and again at 8.45 p.m. outside our sector, the right, there were bursts of hostile fire which lasted about 5 minutes. Our aeroplanes kept the anti-aircraft guns of the enemy employed. One, which flew over our lines at 4.15 p.m., had 79 shells fired at it. (Reported by Infantry).

Our Artillery registered during the day on front near SUNKEN ROAD where enemy post located our patrol the previous evening (Q.4.d.45.35). The bombarded it later - result unknown.
PATROLS.
A patrol went out from our lines at JACOB'S LADDER between 8.30 p.m. and 10.p.m. The patrol found a large working party on SUNKEN ROAD with covering party. Nature of work not ascertained.

INTELLIGENCE.
ENEMY MOVEMENTS.
Several men, probably on fatigue, were seen in BEAUMONT HAMEL.

A working party was observed at about 12.20 at point Q.6.b.36.

A party of about 20 men were observed drilling at 2.50 p.m. at a point 400 yards East of IRLES CHURCH. This continued for 50 minutes.

At 4.30 p.m. a working party was observed at point Q.6.a.5.8.

A working party which seemed to be carrying timber, were observed at point Q.6.a.6.9. and remained in view for 20 minutes.
ENEMY WORK.
Constant movements to and fro observed in BEAUMONT HAMEL passed a spot where railway line is visible. The men were carrying planks, buckets, ladders etc.. 5 men were seen pushing a truck. Others apparently carrying rations.

In front of Q.10.7.8 digging and blasting heard in enemy's trenches at 10.30 p.m.
TRAINS AND TRANSPORT.
The following train movements were observed:-
9.45 to ACHIET-LE-GRAND from BAPAUME.
11.5 to BAPAUME from ACHIET-LE-GRAND.
11.45 to ACHIET=LE-GRAND from BAPAUME.
2.00 to LE-SARS from BAPAUME. Six trucks.

At 11.30 p.m. a train was heard nearing BEAUMONT HAMEL and soon after a sound of timber being unloaded. (Reported by Infantry).

A certain amount of Transport was heard during the night. (Reported by Infantry).

MISCELLANEOUS.
AEROPLANES.
Enemy aeroplanes were rather more active - at least 2 came over our lines and were driven off by our anti-aircraft guns and our aeroplanes.

W. M. Armstrong

5th May, 1916.

Captain,
G.S., 29th Division.

29TH DIVISION DAILY SUMMARY.
for
Period from 6 a.m. 5/5/16 to 6 a.m. 6/5/16.

HEADQUARTERS.
29th DIVISION.
INTELLIGENCE.
No. I.S.33
Date 6/5/16

OPERATIONS.

ARTILLERY.
x b m y
Enemy Artillery shelled the Right Sub-sector briskly during the morning. It was quieter on the Left Sub-sector but a working party on the new Cook-house at Q.9.d.5560. were

Our Artillery retaliated by shelling the trenches about Q.11.a.77.

Our Artillery fired 14 rounds at the listening Post in SUNKEN ROAD about 2 a.m.

PATROLS.
A patrol went out about 1 a.m. from JACOB'S LADDER to reconnoitre the suspected enemy Post on the SUNKEN ROAD(Q.4d) The patrol was fired on again from the same position as on (4.3) the previous occasion. Enemy estimated at 6 Riflemen. These appears to be a permanent listening post here, entrenched and protected by a wire fence. *This post will be bombarded to-night with mortars.*

patrol established the fact that there is

One officer (2/Lt.T.C.Hambling) and one man of the patrol had not returned up to the time of forwarding this report.

A patrol (of 1 N.C.O. and 3 men) examined ground at head of Sap at Q.17.19 (Trench ref.). They reported that the wire there is in fair condition. There is a shell hole and a small disused trench at the end of the Sap. No signs of the enemy were found.

INTELLIGENCE.

ENEMY MOVEMENTS.
Much movement along the road or track in BEAUMONT HAMEL commanded by O.P. at Q.4.8.

Men in light and dark-grey uniform mostly, and white braid on peaked caps (Some wore round flat caps).

One man seen in dark-blue tunic, others with white jackets.

Much traffic observed in trench in front apparently of main positions of HAWTHORN REDOUBT.

Enemy wearing white suits, working on top of CHALK TRENCH on right of road leading to BRANCOURT VILLAGE.

A few men in grey uniforms, with slung rifles but without equipment were seen by the 1st R.I.F. moving from N.E. of BEAUMONT HAMEL, to a stationary water cart on a rough road. The position of the water cart is probably Q.8.d.3.5.

ENEMY WORK.
About 6 men were at work in the trenches near Q.11.c.7.6. Small working parties were observed between points Q.6.a.56, Q.6.a.88 and Q.6.a.82. New earth has been thrown up at intervals between these points, working parties were using logs of wood in their work.

A party of about 200 men was observed, 4 men on horseback in rear, marching on road in direction of GREVILLERS.

TRAINS AND TRANSPORT.
The following train movements were observed:-
4.15 -- to BAPAUME from ACHIET-LE-GRAND
4.45 -- to ACHIET-LE-GRAND from BAPAUME.
5.00 -- to BAPAUME from LE-SARS.

MISCELLANEOUS.

AEROPLANES.
At 4.30 a.m. an enemy 'plane approached our lines but was driven off by our anti-aircraft guns. The same thing occurred at 7 a.m. At 12 noon a third aeroplane was seen to retire on the appearance of one of our aeroplanes.

2.

MISCELLANEOUS.   One of the 2/S.W.B's snipers, on the 4th inst., about 6.45 p.m. fired at German who had exposed himself after working at Q.10.d.77.47. The man fell back and remained in the same condition till nightfall. During the night of 4/5th May, sounds of timber being unloaded and planks and logs being moved about were coming apparently from an enemy communication trench behind the SALIENT in Q.10.d.5.7. The position cannot be more definitely given.

C. Fuller
Lieut. Colonel, G.S

6th May, 1916.   29th Division.

29th DIVISION DAILY SUMMARY.

for

Period from 6.0 am. 6/5/16 to 6.0 am. 7/5/16.

HEADQUARTERS.
29th DIVISION.
INTELLIGENCE.
No. D.S.34
Date 7/5/16

OPERATIONS.   **ARTILLERY.**

The enemy artillery displayed more activity than usual shelling persistently our front line, support and communication trenches, an area between Q.26.3. and the left of the Sector.
Between 3.0 and 4.0 pm. a percussion shrapnel shell grazed the parapet of the South Bay of Q.16.7 and burst immediately, and wounded one man, severely, in the head and slightly wounded two others. The helmet is submitted for examination. The man was still living at 5.0 pm. It was not unlikely that the enemy has observed our working parties.

TRENCH MORTARS.
Our trench mortars fired a few registering rounds at about 7.30 pm. from two emplacements in TENDERLOIN STREET, firing at the enemy's listening posts position on SUNKEN ROAD. Almost immediately the enemy spotted the gun positions and bombarded with "Whizz Bangs" about 15 rounds grazing the high ground behind JACOB'S LADDER to the left of ESAU'S WAY, some falling about 15 yards behind the fire trench, others nearer the T.M. Battery. (Reported by Infantry).

MACHINE GUNS.
Our machine guns at LUNA and BOWERY opened fire in conjunction with the artillery at 12 midnight. Short, sharp bursts were kept up till 1.20 am. when both guns ceased fire on account of information that a patrol was going out from our trenches at 12.30 am.
The shooting of the 18 pdrs. was excellent (Reported by Infantry).

PATROLS.
About 11.0 pm. a patrol (1st R.Inniskilling Fusiliers) examined the ground all round the MARY REDAN and found nothing unusual.
Soon after midnight a strong enemy patrol of about 30 approached our wire by the SUNK ROAD outside Q.16.3. [Trench ref.] and put up flares. They were fired on and returned.
A patrol of 2 Officers and 8 Other Ranks were sent out to examine ground near enemy post on SUNKEN ROAD. Patrol quite successful and found all clear. A natural cup-like hollow exists just beyond the road, the ground being covered with footprints. It is inferred that the listening post has been withdrawn on account of our artillery fire.

INTELLIGENCE.   **ENEMY WORK.**
Heavy blasting again observed opposite Q.10.7-8 at 3.0 am. Steam and smoke observed issuing from same locality. It is suggested that enemy are using steam drills (Reported by Infantry).
Men were seen in BEAUMONT HAMEL dressed in marching order with round caps without peaks and blue-grey greatcoats.
   20 seen at 3.0 pm.
    6 " " 5.30 pm.
    6 " " 6.35 pm.
Other men were seen carrying timber, tins, etc. one riding a bicycle and several pushing trollies along light railway (Reported by Infantry).

2.

SNIPERS.

German snipers, one wearing helmet observed in BEAUMONT HAMEL. One accounted for by our snipers, fell forward out of house. (Reported by Infantry)

ENEMY MOVEMENTS.

Observed a party of about 80 men at point G.22d67 going towards GREVILLERS at 2.5 p.m. Much horse transport was observed passing to and from GREVILLERS at point G.22d67 from 2.30 - 3 p.m. A party of 6 men was observed with slung rifles coming from trench at point Q.6.b.11 disappeared Q.6.b.59 at 4 p.m. A large body of troops about 300 strong was observed at 5.20, 2 horsemen in front 1 horsemen at rear. The flash of the sun on sidearms could be observed, came in view from tree S.E. of IRLES CHURCH. Maps at disposal show roads from point G.32d.30 to G.32c.48.

TRAINS AND TRANSPORT.

The following train movements were observed:=
9.30   BAPAUME to ACHIET-LE-GRAND
10.10 ACHIET-LE-GRAND to BAPAUME
11.00 BAPAUME to LE-SARS.
11.15 BAPAUME to ACHIET-LE-GRAND
11.30   "   "   "   "   "
1.45   BAPAUME to LE-SARS
3.20   BAPAUME to ACHIET-LE-GRAND
4.10   ACHIET-LE-GRAND to BAPAUME
5.45   BAPAUME to ACHIET-LE-GRAND
5.55   ACHIET-LE-GRAND to BAPAUME

MISCELLANEOUS.

AEROPLANES.

Our aeroplanes were active all day and during reconnaisances at 6.30 a.m. and 2.30 p.m. were vigorously shelled.

W. M. Armstrong.

7th May, 1916.

Captain,
G.S., 29th Division.

29th DIVISION DAILY SUMMARY
for
Period from 6 a.m. 7/5/16 to 6 a.m. 8/5/16.

HEADQUARTERS.
29th DIVISION
INTELLIGENCE.
No. D.S.35
Date 8/5/16

OPERATIONS.

ARTILLERY.

During the day the enemy bombarded MARY REDAN and E. end of CONSTITUTION HILL with guns and Trench Mortars, and have filled in the trenches there to a considerable extent. Towards dusk, things were quieter, but at 11 p.m. the enemy fired 6" shells over the lines of the right sub-sector. Our Artillery retaliated and quietness was restored about 12.45 a.m.

Our casualties amounted to 3 Killed and 7 Wounded besides 3 men gased by gas-shells fired about 4 p.m. In the Left sub-sector the enemy registered on Q.10.1 and Q.10.2 (Trench ref.). At 6.15 a.m. with H.E. At 8 a.m. he again registered with 7.7 and shrapnel on Q.16.9 and on the wire between new and old fire trenches. At 5.15 p.m. scattered 50 shrapnel rounds along the front line of the sub-sector. At 10.40 a.m. the enemy artillery showed considerable liveliness with Field Artillery and one Heavy Battery. At 11.45 a.m. our artillery retaliated by bombarding the enemy's lines heavily for an hour. (Reported by Infantry).

TRENCH MORTARS.

In addition to the destruction wrought on MARY REDAN minnenwerfer registered at 8 a.m. on the wire in front of Q.10.1 and Q.10.2 and at 5 p.m. registered in front of and behind the fire trench at Q.16.9. shelled

The report that the enemy shattered our Trench Mortar emplacements mentioned in this summary on the 7th is incorrect. They fired on the old disused positions the guns being purposely changed in order to mislead them.

PATROLS.

A standing patrol of 1 Officer and 1 N.C.O. and 2 men left Sap 5 in the Left Sub-sector at 9 p.m. They proceeded East for about 60 yards when they saw a German standing patrol of 4 men in front of the enemy wire. They also heard the sound of digging at Q.10.b.5.7. Patrol returned at 11.15 p.m.

At 9 p.m. a patrol of 2 N.C.Os. and 2 men went out from our line at JACOB'S LADDER. The patrol got close to the SUNKEN ROAD but was not fired on.

INTELLIGENCE.

EMPLACEMENT.

A Trench Mortar is strongly suspected at Q.11.d.5277.

ENEMY WORK.

M.G. Officers at AUCHONVILLERS report seeing a party of the enemy about 10 men, working on wire in front of BEAUMONT at 8.30 p.m. Fire was opened and party dispersed.

A working party was observed at point Q.6.a.84. New earth has been thrown up at this point. 2 Men were observed looking over top of trench at point Q.5.d.87. One man pointing to objects as if explaining positions.

ENEMY MOVEMENTS.

The usual movement was observed in BEAUMONT HAMEL. One man wearing a white coat, blue cap with red band. Several trolleys observed loading with timber abd tarpaulins.

TRAINS AND TRANSPORT.

The following train movements were observed:-
9.40 from ACHIET-LE-GRAND to BAPAUME
10.   "   "   "   "   "   "   "
10.35 BAPAUME to ACHIET-LE-GRAND
11.10 "   "   "   "   "
11.35 ACHIET-LE-GRAND to BAPAUME
2.20 "   "   "   "   "
2.35 BAPAUME to ACHIET-LE-GRAND
3.30 "   "   "   "   "
3.45 ACHIET-LE-GRAND to BAPAUME
4.15 "   "   "   "   "
4.45 Bapaume to Achiet le Grand
5.15

- 2 -

TRAINS AND TRANSPORT. (Contd.)
5.15 from ACHIET-LE-GRAND to BAPAUME.

SNIPERS.
A sniper's post has been located at Q.10.d.5.8.

MISCELLANEOUS.
FLARES.
Lights red and green were freely used as well as one that on bursting gave out a cone of "Golden Rain" showing for about 3 seconds.

W.M. Armstrong

                Captain, G.S.,
8th May, 1918.   29th Division.

29th DIVISION DAILY SUMMARY.

for

Period from 6 a.m. 8/5/16 to 6 a.m. 9/5/16.

HEADQUARTERS.
29th DIVISION.
INTELLIGENCE.
No. D.S.36
Date. 9/5/16

OPERATIONS.

ARTILLERY.

With the exception of a few whizz bangs directed against the front line of the Left Sector the day passed quite quietly. The Right sub-sector report our artillery as having done some long range shooting during the night.

A few shells were sent into AUCHONVILLERS during the afternoon 8/5/16. Four shells (Shrapnel) also fell there at 8.30 p.m. (8/5/16).

PATROLS.

A standing patrol of 1 Officer, 1 N.C.O. and 4 men, left No.5 Sap at 12.45 a.m. to listen for sounds of working at Q.10.d.55.75. The patrol returned at 2.15 a.m. when the N.C.O. and one man reported that they had heard the sounds of an air-pump.

A patrol under Corporal Dixon (1st Lancashire Fus:) proceeded towards the suspected enemy listening post at SUNKEN ROAD (Q.4.d.4.5). They reported sounds like blows with a hammer or mallet, but as the night was very quiet this probably came from the enemy's wire. The patrol did not proceed to the spot itself, as they had had no opportunity to view the ground in day-light. The 4th Battalion Worcester Regiment reported that a patrol investigated this place further on 7/8th and came to the conclusion that there was no permanent post there.

INTELLIGENCE.

ENEMY WORK.

At Q.10.d.70.50 pick and shovel were audible during the night.

Early on the morning of the 8th instant puffs of smoke such as come from a locomotive were seen issuing from a Sap at the end of Q.10.d.85.75. The sentry thought it was steam.

As fresh earth is constantly being thrown up and wood is heard being dumped there, this steam or smoke may have to do with the mining operations or excavation by mechanical means.

A working party was observed at Q.6.c.7.8.

ENEMY MOVEMENTS.

Much transport (Motor and horse) were observed at G.22.d.6.7 going to and from GREVILLERS.

TRAINS AND TRANSPORT.

The following train movements were observed:-

Time	Movement	Trucks
7.00	to LE-SARS from BAPAUME.	
9.55	to BAPAUME from ACHIET-LE-GRAND	
10.20	to ACHIET-LE-GRAND from BAPAUME.	
11.10	to BAPAUME from ACHIET-LE-GRAND.	
11.25	to " " " "	
12.20	to ACHIET-LE-GRAND from BAPAUME.	
12.45	to BAPAUME to LE-SARS.	18 Trucks.
1.30	" " "	7 Trucks.
2.10	BAPAUME from ACHIET-LE-GRAND.	
3.00	to ACHIET-LE-GRAND from BAPAUME.	
3.20	to " " " " "	
3.45	to BAPAUME from LE-SARS.	8 Trucks.
4.10	to BAPAUME from ACHIET-LE-GRAND.	
5.40	to ACHIET-LE-GRAND from BAPAUME.	

MISCELLANEOUS.

A large white sheet was observed blowing about behind earth-works at point Q.6.a.6.4.

SIGNALS.

(a) Search-light. At about 1.15 a.m. on the 8th instant a double search-light in the shape of a V was noticed sweeping from side to side. It seemed to be situated a considerable distance South of our line behind the enemy front. A compass bearing/

SIGNALS. (Cont'd)
bearing was taken from Q.10.c.20.40 on the search-light and found to be 171° Magnetic.
    (b) It is believed by the Infantry (2/S.W.B.) now holding the Left Sub-sector that the signal for enemy Machine Gun to traverse our lines is a <u>White</u> flare followed by a <u>Green</u> one.

[signature]

Lieut.Colonel, G.S.,

9th May, 1916.
                                  29th Division.

29th DIVISION DAILY SUMMARY.
for
Period from 6 a.m. 9/5/16 to 6 a.m. 10/5/16.

OPERATIONS.

ARTILLERY.

The enemy paid more attention to the Left Sub-sector than to the Right. From 11.30 a.m. to 12.15 p.m. he fired about 100 shells on the parapet of the new trench and the parados of the original fire trench between 1st Avenue and "B" Street. He fired an occasional salvo of shrapnel at parties working in the Right Sub-Sector, but otherwise was quiet in this Sector.

At 12.15 p.m. 9/5/16 twelve shrapnel shells were fired on one of our batteries near AUCHONVILLERS. Our guns sent a few shells into BEAUMONT HAMEL during the day. The enemy Artillery shelled the Left Sub-sector trenches at intervals, doing no damage.

TRENCH MORTARS.

About 20 T.M. Shells fell in our wire in front of Left Sub-sector about 7.30 a.m.

PATROLS.

The REDAN was patrolled all through the night but there was nothing to report.

From 8.30 p.m. to 2 a.m. a standing patrol of 1 N.C.O. and 2 men were out in front of the wire opposite Q.10.d.55.70 and heard digging going on at the end of the communication trench at that point. The patrol was fired on but no one was hit.

A patrol 2/Lt. Uren (1st Lancashire Fus:) investigated the suspected enemy listening posts near the SUNKEN ROAD but reported all clear.

A listening patrol on coming back to the line was fired on.

RAID.

Preparations were made to meet an expected raid on the Right of our line. There was no sign of it.

INTELLIGENCE.

ENEMY WORK.

Fatigue parties were seen behind HAWTHORN REDOUBT emptying bags of chalk. About 7.30 a.m. 2 Germans were seen 1000 yards away, collecting old sand bags on the parapet. Two shots were fired and they ran into the trench.

SNIPERS.

It is believed that a German who exposed himself by looking over the parapet at Q.10.b.55.70 was shot by one of our snipers at 6.45 p.m.

TRAINS AND TRANSPORT.

Much transport (Horse) was observed at G.22.d.6.7.
A steam roller (Road) came into view at M.2.b.8.3 and stopped at M.2..b.6.8.

The following train movements were observed:-

```
10.00 to ACHIET-LE-GRAND from BAPAUME
10.5    "       "       "    "    "
10.30   "       "       "    "    "
11.10   BAPAUME from ACHIET-LE-GRAND
 3.45      "     "      "
 5.15   ACHIET-LE-GRAND from BAPAUME
 5.45       "       "    "    "
 5.55   BAPAUME from ACHIET-LE-GRAND.
```

MISCELLLANEOUS./

MISCELLANEOUS.

AEROPLANES.
One of our aeroplanes flew over the enemy's lines at 10 a.m. but was not fired on.

FIRES.
At 9.30 p.m. a large fire was observed from Q.16.b.30.85 to be burning behind the enemy's lines at what was estimated to be a distance of over 5 miles at about 110° Magnetic.

FLARES.
A bright flare was noticed behind BEAUMONT HAMEL about 9.30 p.m. yesterday. It died down but was noticed again at intervals.

At 12.35 p.m. 9/5/16 white flare-lights rising from PUISIEUX-au-MONT were observed at point R.1.b.5.2.

Most of the flares sent up from the enemy lines came from the communication trench at Q.10.d.53.70.

W.M. Armstrong

10th May, 1916.

Captain, G.S.,
29th Division.

29th DIVISION DAILY SUMMARY.

For Period From

6 a.m. 10/5/16 to 6 a.m. 11/5/16.

HEADQUARTERS.
29th DIVISION.
INTELLIGENCE.
No. D.S. 38
Date 11/5/16

OPERATIONS.

ARTILLERY.

The situation was on the whole quiet. One isolated Howitzer H.E. Shell dropped near LIMERICK JUNCTION, killing one man, and injuring two men of the 87th Brigade Machine Gun Company. There was a brisk firing on our right some distance away, at 11 a.m. and again between 2 a.m. and daybreak.

About 12 shots were fired at one of our working parties at Q.10/17 about 10.45 p.m. on the 10/5/16. A few shells were fired on Q.10.8 about 1 p.m. Our Artillery were registering on the HAWTHORN REDOUBT at intervals during the day, and we fired several heavy shells there between 1 a.m. and 3 a.m. 11/5/16.

MACHINE GUNS.

Enemy Machine Guns were active against aeroplanes during the day and one fired a burst at a working party in LANWICK STREET (Q.4/7.) about 11 p.m. 10/5/16.

PATROLS.

MARY REDAN was patrolled during the night, sounds of enemy engaged in wiring were reported.

A patrol went out in front of the Left Sub-sector (Q.10/6.). They could hear the enemy repairing wire and unloading timber in BEAUMONT. This seems to be done nearly every night. A patrol 2/Lieut. Pearson, L/Cpl. Kirwin and 3 men left the Right Sub-sector at 9.50 p.m., 10/5/16, from NEWTOWNWARDS (Q.10/13.). The patrol went half-right, they heard stakes being driven in and wiring along line opposite Q.10.12 to Q.10.6.

A pump working with metallic clank was also heard.

Later several forms were seen and an enemy patrol was noticed in front. We turned a Machine Gun on to their wiring party which retired. The enemy patrol also retired.

At 1.45 a.m. 11/5/16, we sent out another patrol from HAPPY ALLEY (Q.10/14.), which went half-right to the crest of the ridge, hiding the enemy line. Wiring by the enemy appeared to have ceased though pumping again was heard.

INTELLIGENCE.

ENEMY MOVEMENTS.

Observers of the 2nd S.W.B. report that the uniforms and clothing of the enemy opposite their section are cleaner and smarter than formally. This suggested to mean that reliefs or reinforcements have recently taken place. These observations are being continued.

WIRE.

New wire has been observed on the South Side of SALIENT in Q.10.d.

TRAINS AND TRANSPORT.

Sixteen Horse Transport Wagons were seen coming from GREVILLERS on road at point G.22.d.6.7. 12 Horse Transport Wagons were seen on road at G.33.b.4.3.

Horse transport was also observed coming from PYS on road at point M.2.c.26.

The steam road roller reported May, 9th is now lying on road at point G.33.b.74. This road from the above mentioned point to G.34.a.77 seems to be undergoing repair at night.

The following train movements were observed:-

9.45 /

TRAINS AND TRANSPORT. (Cont^d.)

```
 9.45  to ACHIET-LE-GRAND from BAPAUME
10.30  to      "      "    "      "
11.00  to BAPAUME from ACHIET-LE-GRAND
11.15  to    "      "       "
11.45  to BAPAUME from LE-SARS          14 Trucks.
 1.00  to ACHIET-LE-GRAND from BAPAUME
 3.47  to      "      "    "      "
 5.15  to BAPAUME from LE-SARS           9 Trucks.
 5.15  to BAPAUME from ACHIET-LE-GRAND
 6.00  to    "      "       "
```

MISCELLANEOUS:

SIGNALS.

A light from several hundred yards behind the enemy's line opposite Q.10.11 is constantly seen. It is sent up very straight and high.

BALLOONS.

A stationary Balloon was observed at 60° Magnetic from ENGLEBELMER CHURCH.

A Balloon was noticed from THE BOS - de - LOGEAST WOOD at 3.45 p.m. 10/5/16. and descended at 10.5 p.m.

EXPLOSION.

At 8 p.m. two slight explosions were heard from an enemy trench about Q.10.d.80.40. A cloud of smoke and vapour was observed to issue from the trench.

At 5 p.m. and again after mid-night distinct earth tremor was felt, possibly due to distant mines.

C.G. Fuller.
Lieut. Colonel, G.S.,
29th Division.

11th May, 1916.

29th DIVISION DAILY SUMMARY.
For Period From
6 a.m. 11/5/16 to 6 a.m. 12/5/16.

HEADQUARTERS.
29th DIVISION.
INTELLIGENCE.
No. D.S.39
Date 12/5/16

OPERATIONS.

ARTILLERY. than usual

More activity ~~than recently~~ was shewn by the enemy in the afternoon. He ranged on the old and new firing line between LIMERICK JUNCTION and Q.10.1 (Trench Ref.). Only slight damage was done. In the Right Sub-sector the enemy ranged on our new firing trench on the left of Q.16/2 - 6 and fired some shrapnel behind Battalion Headquarters. At 10.45 p.m. he again shelled working parties on extreme left of the Sector in the new trenches Q.16/6 but only for 5 minutes and without causing casualties.

At about 1.30 p.m. 4 shells (2 failing to explode) were fired at the BOWERY Q.3.d.8.6.

The enemy shelled the trenches in area Q.10.a.b. at 11.30 p.m. presumably searching for working parties. Our Artillery shelled the enemy's trenches in area Q.10.b., three times during the night 11/12th.

MACHINE GUNS.

An emplacement has been noted at Q.4.d.88.09. This has been observed and report will be confirmed later.

A machine gun is reported to have fired at our aeroplane from Q.17.a.97.70.

TRENCH MORTARS.

At 6.15 p.m. 2 Minenwerfer bombs, dropped just outside MARY REDAN.

PATROLS.

Two patrols left the Left Sub-sector Q.16/7 to Q.10/7. One heard wiring on North of SALIENT at Q.10.d.55.70.

The SUNKEN ROAD and BEAUMONT ROADS were patrolled last night. The enemy were wiring at HAWTHORN REDOUBT.

A patrol left our line at Q.10.10 and patrolled NO MAN'S LAND up to the SUNKEN ROAD opposite Q.4/2. No enemy patrols were seen.

INTELLIGENCE.

ENEMY WORK.

Between 4 and 4.30 p.m. smoke and dust were seen rising from support trench at Q.11.c.10.78; the same phenomena again at 5.30 a.m. in the same place. It may be a cook-house. The SALIENT here is being carefully watched.

Observed a working party at point Q.6.a.24.90.

ENEMY MOVEMENTS.

About 50 men passed a point in BEAUMONT HAMEL between 6 and 7 p.m. in full marching order and carrying white sacks.

TRAINS AND TRANSPORT.

Much Horse Transport was observed at 7.45 a.m. passing to and from PYS, on road at point N.1.d.73.

A party of about 30 men were observed going towards GREVILLERS on road at point G.22d.8.7.

The following train movements were observed:-

8.15 to	ACHIET-LE-GRAND from BAPAUME.	
9.20 to	" " " " "	
10.0 to	BAPAUME from ACHIET-LE-GRAND	
11.45 to	" " " " "	
11.20	ACHIET-LE-GRAND from BAPAUME	
13.30	LE-SARS from BAPAUME	5 Trucks
4.45	ACHIET-LE-GRAND from BAPAUME	9 Covered Trucks
5.00	BAPAUME from LE-SARS	10 Trucks.

MISCELLANEOUS./

MISCELLANEOUS.

SIGNALS.
A bright white flare went up vertically behind BEAUMONT, going out after one flash of light. This was followed within 5 seconds by a burst of shrapnel at the Right Sub-sector.

BALLOONS.
Two balloons were observed near the Wood BOIS de LOGEAST between 7 a.m. and 9 a.m. 11/5/16. Another was observed over BUCQUOY.

The enemy has placed a white screen in the parapet at Q.4.d.9.4.

12th May, 1916.

Captain, G.S.,
29th Division.

29th DIVISION DAILY SUMMARY.
For Period From
6 a.m. 12/5/16 to 6 a.m. 13/5/16.

HEADQUARTERS,
29th DIVISION.
INTELLIGENCE.

No. D.S.40
Date. 13/5/16

OPERATIONS.

ARTILLERY.

The enemy shewed considerable activity throughout the period. Between 11 a.m. and Noon about 50 shells (7.5) landed in the area between Q.16.6 and Q.10.3, about 50 yards behind the existing line.

The trenches in the Left Sub-sector were shelled at various points yesterday between 8 a.m. and 9 a.m., little damage being done. Fourteen heavy shells were fired at the BOWERY between 10 and 11 a.m., the majority falling short.

Our Artillery fired 8 shells at a sniper's post at Q.10.d.55.70.

MACHINE GUNS.

At about 1 a.m. Machine Guns traversed the front line of the Left Sub-sector. Lewis Gun fire in reply was aimed at Q.10.d.80.75 from which the M.G. fire was suspected to come.

PATROLS.

A standing patrol left Q.16.6 at 9 p.m. and patrolled Sap 6 going out about 80 yards. It returned at 11.30 p.m. having seen nothing unusual.

INTELLIGENCE.

ENEMY WORK.

At 9 a.m. enemy were seen leaving their trenches at point Q.5.c.5.6 and seemed to start wiring. They were only visible for five minutes and their movements were hurried. They wore blue trousers and were in shirt sleeves.

ENEMY MOVEMENTS.

At 6.30 p.m. four Germans were seen walking down a slope about Q.12.a.3.2. Two wore whiteish tunics and two dark tunics and whiteish breeches. All wore round blue or black caps.

An enemy observer was noticed at Q.10.b.80.75. Puffs of smoke were constantly seen at Q.5.c.1.5. There appears to be a machine there, probably a mechanical excavator.

TRAINS AND TRANSPORT.

Much transport was noticed going to and from GREVILLERS. At 9 p.m. and 10.30 p.m. transport and trains could be heard close up to the enemy's front line to the S.W. of BEAUMONT HAMEL &

A steam roller (Road) was observed going towards GREVILLERS, at 10.30 on road at point G.22.d.6.7.

The following train movements were observed:-

7.30 to LE-SARS from BAPAUME.
10.00 to ACHIET-LE-GRAND from BAPAUME.
10.15 to " " " " "
11.15 to BAPAUME from ACHIET-LE-GRAND.
11.45 to " " " " "
12.30 to ACHIET-LE-GRAND from BAPAUME.
4.35 to " " " " "
5.58 to BAPAUME from ACHIET-LE-GRAND.

MISCELLANEOUS.

RELIEF.

There was a marked increase on rifle fire during the night and young men have been seen exposing themselves while pointing out parts of our line. From this it may be inferred that a relief in this Sector has taken place.

AEROPLANES.

Our aeroplanes scouted all day and were fired on with Machine Guns without apparently the slightest effect.

W. M. Armstrong

Captain, G.S.,
29th Division.

13th May, 1916.

29th DIVISION DAILY SUMMARY.
For Period From
6 a.m. 13/5/16 to 6 a.m. 14/5/16.

HEADQUARTERS
29th DIVISION
INTELLIGENCE
No. D.S.41
Date 14/5/16

OPERATIONS.

ARTILLERY.

The enemy bombarded the trenches round about PICADILLY and CONSTITUTION HILL with about 20 rounds of small shrapnel and at 12.15 p.m. GABION AVENUE about the point Q.16.c.6.7.

The enemy Artillery was on the whole quiet. The front line trenches North of NEW BEAUMONT ROAD were shelled. Some damage was done to the parapet which has since been repaired. The BOWERY was shelled without any damage being done.

MACHINE GUNS.

A Machine Gun fired at JACOB'S LADDER and to the North of it from Q.4.d.88.09.

At 8.30 p.m. on the 12th instant an enemy Machine Gun traversed the road from ENGLEBELMER to MESNIL at the point Q.21.c.8.1 backwards and forwards for a short distance for about 5 minutes. Almost immediately afterwards a large amount of transport passed this spot.

PATROLS.

Patrols were out in reliefs from 9 p.m. to 2 a.m. North of NEW BEAUMONT ROAD but had nothing to report. A Listening Post on the SUNKEN ROAD Q.4.d.4.3 reported no signs of enemy's patrols but rather more rifle fire than usual.

INTELLIGENCE.

ENEMY MOVEMENTS.

A party of troops about 40 strong were seen going towards PYS on road at point M.1.d.69.

About 3 p.m. 13/5/16 a party of 20 men were seen in BEAUMONT HAMEL each with about 3 yards of wire bound hose-pipe. They were going towards HAWTHORN REDOUBT.

TRAINS AND TRANSPORT.

The following train movements were observed:-
10.15 to BAPAUME from ACHIET-LE-GRAND.
10.30 to LE-SARS from BAPAUME.
10.32 to BAPAUME from ACHIET-LE-GRAND.
2.20 to BAPAUME from LE-SARS
3.30 to " "   10 Trucks.
3.45 to BAPAUME from ACHIET-LE-GRAND.
4.30 to ACHIET-LE-GRAND from BAPAUME.

Much horse transport was seen going to and from GREVILLERS on road at point G.22.d.6.7.

MISCELLANEOUS.

AEROPLANES.

Our Aeroplanes were active during the while of yesterday and again at 5 a.m. to-day.

WELLS.

A Civilian in ENGLEBELMER who knows BEAUMONT HAMEL says that the wells in the latter village are all sunk very deep and are apt to run short of water in late summer. When this happens the inhabitants prefer to cart water from BEAUCOURT sur ANCRE rather than run the risk of exhausting their wells.

SMOKE.

Smoke was seen rising from trenches at points Q.5.c.37 and Q.5.a.45 respectively.

SEARCHLIGHT.

A searchlight was noticed well behind BEAUMONT HAMEL on 12/5/16, and the bearing of 125° Magnetic from Q.10.7/8.

DUMP.

A dump is suspected in a hollow about Q.11.d.10.90, owing to increased noise and transport heard there. A fuse was found in

- 2 -

in Q.10.a. marked:-

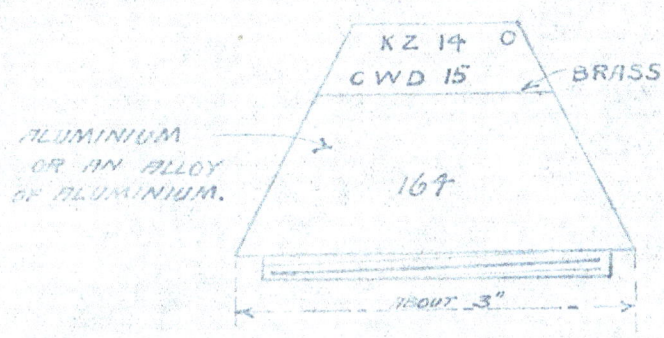

W. M. Armstrong

Captain, G.S.,
29th Division.

14th May, 1916.

29th DIVISION DAILY SUMMARY.
For Period From
6 a.m. 14/5/16 to 6 a.m. 15/5/16.

> HEADQUARTERS.
> 29th DIVISION.
> INTELLIGENCE.
> No. DS 42
> Date 15/5/16

OPERATIONS.
ARTILLERY.

In our Right Sector the enemy fired Twenty 7.7 shells at our front trenches during the morning, without doing any damage.

Between 2 and 2.30 p.m. four or five rounds H.E. fell close to the entrance of TIPPERARY AVENUE. Again at 4.30 p.m. Fifteen 7.7mm. shells came over Q.16.4 but did no damage, in reply our Artillery fired shrapnel and H.E. at the enemy's wire on South side of SALIENT in G.10.d. In the morning between 10.30 and 11.30 our Artillery ranged on the road between BEAUMONT HAMEL and BEAUCOURT with H.E..

On our Left Sector there was little activity. The enemy shelled the line yesterday at Q.4.7/8 doing no damage. Several shells in S.W. part of MAILLY-MAILLET, P.12.d. about 1 p.m Heavy Artillery fire was heard about 10.45 p.m. some distance to our right.

PATROLS.

Patrols were out from 10 p.m. to mid-night along the SUNKEN ROAD (Q.4.d.) They examined our wire, and reported no signs of enemy patrols.

INTELLIGENCE.
ENEMY WORK.

New stakes have been placed in front of the trench from Q.6.a.25.90 to a point North of PENDANT COPSE. At 10.15 a.m. a party of 10 men was observed on the road to PYS apparently working on the road.

At 3.30 earth was being thrown up at point Q.6.c.77.

ENEMY MOVEMENTS.

At 2 p.m. a considerable amount of Horse Transport was observed at G.22.d.67 apparently proceeding to and from GREVILLERS At 3.32 p.m. a party of 40 men was observed going towards GREVILLERS at point G.22.d.6.7.

TRAINS AND TRANSPORT.

The following train movements were observed:-
11.50 to BAPAUME from LE-SARS
12.25 to BAPAUME from ACHIET-LE-GRAND.
 3.45 to   "   "   "   "
 5.00 to ACHIET-LE-GRAND from BAPAUME.

MISCELLANEOUS.
AEROPLANES.

Our Aeroplanes were active all day long. At 7.20 p.m. a Taube appeared from the North flying very high but returned in the same direction on our Anti-aircraft guns opening fire.

FLARES.

The enemy have used very few flares during the last 2 or 3 nights as compared with the previous week or two.

15th May, 1916.

Captain, G.S.,
29th Division.

29th DIVISION DAILY SUMMARY.
For Period From
6 a.m. 15/5/16 to 6 a.m. 16/5/16.

HEADQUARTERS.
29th DIVISION.
INTELLIGENCE.

No. D.S. 43
Date 16/5/16

OPERATIONS.

ARTILLERY.

At 10.30 a.m. the enemy fired 14 rounds (7·7cm) in the region of the new trench and PICCADILLY. The bombardment lasted for an hour and a quarter, but did no damage. At 2.30 p.m. he fired 12 more rounds of the same kind into the same area again, without damage. At 3.35 p.m. he bombarded UXBRIDGE ROAD and CONSTITUTION HILL with 30 rounds 7·7 and 18 rounds of what was estimated to be 15 cm. During this bombardment he scored three 3 direct hits in CONSTITUTION HILL which damaged the Parados, otherwise the fire was without effect. Our Artillery replied in the area Q.11.c. and Q.17.a.and b. An enemy Battery was observed at about 3.30 p.m. to be firing from behind trees at a point in R.20.A. which cannot as yet be more accuately determined.

At 12.20 a.m. the enemy commenced a heavy bombardment the greatest volume of which seemed to be directed on the part of our line well to the North of our Sector. The parts within the Sector affected were Q.10.6 and neighbourhood, and Q.16.6, from Q.16.6 to Q.17.12.

Our Artillery shelled the enemy trenches North of BEAUMONT HAMEL yesterday afternoon. A few shells fell in AUCHONVILLERS during the day doing no damage. During the bombardment which took place at 12.30 a.m. North of our Area several shells fell in AUCHONVILLERS. They were of small calibre and many failed to explode.

MACHINE GUNS.

At about 8.p.m. 15/5/16 a machine gun opened fire on 2nd AVENUE near the AUCHONVILLERS end. An Officer and 2 men were wounded.

MINNENWERFER., took part in the bombardment, at 12.30 A.M and deposited from 20 - 30 Large Bombs in the Region of Q.10.4 and Q.16.7.

No movement of the enemy was observed. The bombardment slackened off at about 1.20 a.m. and quiet was restored at 2 a.m. Only 5 Casualties have been reported so far and no damage was done to the defences. Our Artillery replied.

PATROLS.

A patrol formed the listening post on the SUNKEN ROAD and later patrolled this road. The unloading of carts was heard in BEAUMONT HAMEL.

INTELLIGENCE. WORK.

ENEMY MOVEMENTS.

A party was observed to be working in a second line trench in the rear of HAWTHORN REDOUBT about 1.5 p.m. in Q.11.a. The point cannot be fixed with more precision.

A small trench has been dug from point Q.6.c.35 to Q.6.c.64..

ENEMY MOVEMENTS.

18 men were observed on the road going towards PYS.

TRAINS AND TRANSPORT.

Much Horse transport was seen passing to and from PYS.
The following train movements were observed:-
10.30 to BAPAUME from ACHIET-LE-GRAND.
11.45 to ACHIET-LE-GRAND from BAPAUME.
12.30 to   "   "   "   "   "
 2.5 to BAPAUME from ACHIET-LE-GRAND.
 3.15 to ACHIET-LE-GRAND from BAPAUME.
 3.45 to BAPAUME from ACHIET-LE-GRAND.
 4.20 to ACHIET-LE-GRAND from BAPAUME.
 4.30 to BAPAUME from LE-SARS   7 Trucks.
 4.45 to ACHIET-LE-GRAND from BAPAUME.
 5.30 to LE-SARS from BAPAUME.

MISCELLANEOUS

MISCELLANEOUS.

A wiring party in front of the unfinished portion of new firing line Q.10.3 and Q.10.4. detected an enemy Patrol and fired on it. The enemy retired without replying to the fire. This occurred at 12.10a.m. i.e. about 10 minutes before the Bombardment started.

SIGNALS.

(1) At 11.30 p.m. a red light was seen to rise from the direction of BEAUMONT HAMEL followed by a Green Rocket which broke into Two parts and was visible for about 30 seconds.

(2) The Bombardment at 12.20 a.m. was immediately preceded by the appearance of a red light and a white light sent up from the direction of BEAUMONT HAMEL. A red Light from the same quarters immediately preceded the cessation of fire. (Reported by Infantry).

AEROPLANES.

There was less aeroplane activity than usual.

TIMBER.

It has been noticed that nearly all the timber seen carried in BEAUMONT HAMEL goes from South to North towards the REDOUBT.

Lieut.Colonel, G.S.,
29th Division.

16th May, 1916.

29th DIVISION DAILY SUMMARY.
For Period From
6 a.m. 16/5/16 to 6 a.m. 17/5/16.

HEADQUARTERS.
29th DIVISION.
INTELLIGENCE.
No. D.S. 44
Date 17/5/16

OPERATIONS.

ARTILLERY.

In our Right Sector the enemy fired 2 - 7.7mm. shells over PICCADILLY and 14 also similar H.E. shells over ESSEX STREET one of which blew in part of the end M.G. emplacement in ESSEX STREET just North of the Sector Boundary, no damage was done.

In Left Sector the enemy fired a few 5.9 H.E. shells in Q.13.a. & b West of MAILLY MAILLET at about 12.30 p.m. Our Artillery fired on and silenced a machine gun which was firing from about Q.4.d.8.5.

MACHINE GUNS.

The enemy was fairly active during the night firing along our front from Q.10.6 to Q.10.7 inclusive.

At midnight on our Left Sector all the Brigade Machine Guns opened fire on the enemy's front Line and barbed wire. A short burst of fire was opened 5 minutes later followed by a final burst at 12.10 a.m.

The enemy sent up a Green Light and replied vigorously with Machine Gun fire. At 15 the enemy fired about 8 small shells in the vicinity of Q.10.10 and Q.10.15, no damage was done.

TRENCH MORTARS.

Our Trench Mortars near PILK STREET registered on Y Ravine at 3.50 p.m. The enemy's Artillery retaliated with a few rounds.

PATROLS.

A Patrol went out between 8.50 p.m. and 10.45 p.m.; made a thorough examination of the SUNKEN ROAD in front of Q.16.3 to find out whether sniping or listening posts had been established there but found no evidence of such. Another patrol examined 2 small dis-used trenches about 100 yards from Q.4.17. No signs of recent occupation were noticed.

INTELLIGENCE.

ENEMY MOVEMENTS.

At 10.30 a.m. a considerable amount of Horse Transport was observed at M.1.d.6.9 apparently proceeding to and from PYS

At 12.45 Horse Transport was observed proceeding towards GREVILLERS at G.22.d.6.7.

At 4.5 p.m. 2 Large horse wagons were observed at G.22.d.6.7 apparently heavy laden with timber coming from the direction of GREVILLERS.

At 4.40 p.m. a large party of troops estimated at about 300 strong was observed proceeding from direction of GREVILLERS. The party passed from view at G.22 A 1.5.

TRAINS AND TRANSPORT.

The following train movements were observed:-
10.25 to ACHIET-LE-GRAND from BAPAUME.
11.5 to BAPAUME from ACHIET-LE-GRAND.
11.15 to   "   "   "   "   "
11.25 to   "   "   "   "   "
12.00 to ACHIET-LE-GRAND from BAPAUME.
2.10 to BAPAUME from LE-SARS
5.5 to ACHIET-LE-GRAND from BAPAUME.

MISCELLANEOUS.

AEROPLANES.

Our Aeroplanes were active all day, they were heavily shelled but without effect. An Aeroplane was heard passing over our lines from the direction of the enemy at 9.30p.m. and appeared to return further South at 10.50 p.m.

17th May, 1916.

Captain, G.S.
29th Division.

29th DIVISION DAILY SUMMARY.
For Period From
6 a.m. 17/5/16 to 6 a.m. 18/5/16.

HEADQUARTERS,
29th DIVISION,
INTELLIGENCE.
No. Q.S.45
Date. 18/5/16

OPERATIONS.

ARTILLERY.

Enemy Artillery was silent on the front, except against our aeroplanes. Some shells, one out of every three of which did not explode were observed to drop near the ENGLEBELMER - AUCHONVILLERS ROAD in Q.14 during the morning. (Reported by Infantry Officers).

Our Artillery kept up desultory fire most of the day. The night was comparatively quiet.

MACHINE GUNS.

Machine Guns swept our wire and front line parapets in the same area as reported yesterday, viz from Q.16/7 to Q.10/6.

At 8.15 p.m. the enemy traversed a machine gun on to AUCHONVILLERS. Our machine gun in AUCHONVILLERS replied and the enemy gun stopped.

PATROLS.

2/Lt. Pyper, 1st Lancashire Fusiliers and 2/Lt. Uren proceeded with patrols at 9 p.m along the SUNKEN ROAD. An enemy patrol fired on them about 11.30 p.m. and 2/Lt. Pyper was wounded. The other Officer (2Lt.Uren) is reported missing. A detailed report will be forwarded when more information is received.

INTELLIGENCE.

ENEMY WORK.

At 2.30 p.m. a party of about 30 without arms were observed to cross the railway line in rear of BEAUCOURT.

ENEMY MOVEMENTS.

In the vicinity of HAWTHORN REDOUBT a certain amount of movement was visible in the trenches as if men were engaged in cleaning them. Sounds of metal being moved about were heard coming from the SALIENT opposite Q.10/4.

At 12.30 p.m. severl Horse Limbers were seen to enter BEAUCOURT. At 9 p.m. and at 11.p.m. heavy transport was heard on the STATION ROAD including Motor Transport. (Reported by M.G.Co:)

SNIPERS.

A sniper fires from somewhere between two trees about Q.5.c.05.60. The exact place has not yet been located.

TRAINS AND TRANSPORT.

The following train movements were observed:-
10.30 to ACHIET-LE-GRAND from BAPAUME.
11.15 to BAPAUME from ACHIET-LE-GRAND.
12.30 to ACHIET-LE-GRAND from BAPAUME.
1.35 to   "   "   "   "   "
1.50 to   "   "   "   "   "
3.00 to   "   "   "   "   "

MISCELLANEOUS.

AEROPLANES.

A hostile aeroplane flew over our lines at 8.30 a.m. but was driven off by our anti-aircraft guns. Between 11 p.m. and 12 Mid-night an aeroplane flew over the MOULIN REDOUBT and dropped a red light between ENGLEBELMER and MAILLY-MAILLET.

SIGNALS.

At 10.15 p.m. three red flares were sent up from a point East of LIMERICK JUNCTION, but nothing followed. At 11 p.m. the same thing happened, also without any apparent consequences.

Lieut: Colonel, G.S.,
29th Division.

18th May, 1916.

20th DIVISION DAILY SUMMARY.
For period from
6 a.m. 18/5/16 to 6 a.m. 19/5/16.

HEADQUARTERS,
20th DIVISION.
INTELLIGENCE.
No. D.S. 46
Date 19/5/16

OPERATIONS.

ARTILLERY.

On our Right Sector a few 77mm. shells were fired at AUCHONVILLERS MILL between 7 and 10 a.m., otherwise the enemy's artillery was practically inactive.

On the Left Sector at 4.20 p.m. our Artillery fired about 8 shells and dispersed a working party, in trench at Q.6.c.80.41, the party dispersed. At 9.15 p.m. the enemy fired a few shrapnel shells over the trench North of the NEW BEAUMONT ROAD.

TRENCH MORTARS.

The enemy fired about 5 or 6 rounds at different times during the night chiefly on the left of our Left Sector.

PATROLS.

On our Left Sector a patrol went out at 9.45 p.m. from Q.4.d.25.80 to the SUNKEN ROAD and returned with the body of a German, who had been killed by our patrol on the previous night.

At 11.30 p.m. another patrol visited the NEW ER ROAD and returned without having encountered the enemy.

On our Left Sector on 17th inst. a patrol went out at 12.30 a.m. and established itself in the SUNKEN ROAD and remained there throughout the night and following day, returning at 9.30 p.m.. No hostile patrols were encountered. A good view of the enemy's wire and trenches was obtained.

On 17th inst. at 10 p.m. one of our patrols again proceeded to the SUNKEN ROAD. Shortly after this the patrol and visiting party was fired on by the enemy. 2/Lt. Pyper was being wounded - 2/Lt. Cran is missing. The patrol was then left in charge of a Corporal. About 4.15 a.m. a hostile patrol approached our patrol and fire was opened at the enemy, killing a German, who has since been identified as

Unter Offizier K.A. Lehmann, Brg. R.Res. Inf.Regts 119
No. 7 Company.

This unter offizier was decorated with the 2nd Class Iron Cross.

INTELLIGENCE.

ENEMY MOVEMENT.

Transport was heard on the BEAUCOURT STATION ROAD from 8.30 p.m. to 11 p.m.

ENEMY WIRE.

New earth has been thrown up at Q.5.c.2.9.
At 3.30 p.m. a working party was observed in the trench at Q.5.b.81.

TRAINS AND TRANSPORT.

The following train movement was observed:-
11.8 to ACHIET-LE-GRAND from BAPAUME.

MISCELLANEOUS.

AEROPLANES.

Our aeroplanes were active, they were shelled without effect.

19th May, 1916.

Captain,
20th Division.

D.S.47.
20/5/16.

29th DIVISION DAILY SUMMARY.
for
Period From 6.0.a.m. on 19/5/16 to 6.0.a.m. on 20/5/16.

OPERATIONS.

Artillery.   On our right sector the enemy fired 7 shrapnel shells at 11.15.a.m. in the vicinity of Q.10.3. doing no damage. On the left sector at 12 noon the enemy fired 30 rounds H.E. in the vicinity of BROADWAY, three men of a working party being wounded. The parapet at Q.10.11. was slightly damaged. At 3.30.p.m. 7 seven shrapnel shells were fired on to the transport approach W. of WHITE CITY. During the afternoon our artillery registered on Y Ravine.

Machine Guns.   A machine gun is suspected to be in position at Q.4.d.85.3.

Patrols.   At 9.30.p.m. our Standing Patrol in the SUNKEN ROAD was attacked by a hostile patrol which tried to surround it. Rifle shots and bombs were exchanged at short range. The hostile patrol disappeared after about 15 minutes. There were no casualties among our men, the officer in charge of our patrols claims to have wounded a German with his revolver. A patrol which left our lines at 9.0.p.m. from Q.10.7. reported that digging was heard opposite Q.10.9. On our right sector a patrol examined the enemy's wire at Q.17.a.96. and reports it to be badly damaged and that a hostile patrol was heard visiting the enemy's sentries. The line appeared to be weakly held here.

INTELLIGENCE.

Enemy Work.   On the right sector small parties were reported to be working on the support and reserve lines.

Enemy Movements.   At 8.40.a.m. a small working party was observed, also steam rising, as if from a small engine or cooker at Q.6.a.80.100.

At 12.20.p.m. four horse transport were observed at G.22.d.6.7. coming from the direction of GREVILLERS.

At 3.15.p.m. a working party was observed in a trench at Q.6.b.21.

Train Transport.   The following train movements were observed:-
12.0.   To ACHIET-LE-GRAND from BAPAUME.

MISCELLANEOUS.

Aeroplanes.   At 9.45.a.m. sentries reported a hostile aeroplane over our lines, it was pursued by two of our aeroplanes and brought down in flames beyond THIEPVAL WOOD.

During the day a notice board appeared in the enemy's line with the following writing on it "Lieut. UREN is dead and buried. What about VISHOF LEHMAN?". A board is being put up in our line today stating that Lehman is dead and buried.

20th May 1916.

Captain, G.S.
29th Division.

29th DIVISION DAILY SUMMARY.
For Period From
6 a.m. 20/5/16 to 6 a.m. 21/5/16.

HEADQUARTERS,
29th DIVISION,
INTELLIGENCE.
No. D.S. 48
Date 21/5/16

OPERATIONS.
ARTILLERY.
On our Left Sector during the day the enemy fired shrapnel at ST. HELEN'S STREET and at communication trenches at Q.10.c; our Artillery registered on the junction of the roads at Q.5.d.8.2 also on the front line trenches at "Y" Ravine. On the Right Sector the enemy registered near LIMERICK JUNCTION.

Between 9 and 9.30 p.m. the enemy fired about 20 rounds of shrapnel over the front line North of NEW BEAUMONT ROAD. This was preceded by the 2 red lights. Our Artillery replied with about 12 rounds shrapnel.

PATROLS.
On our Right Sector a patrol went out from Q.10/6.6 and returned reporting nothing unusual.

A patrol examined the enemy's wire at Q.17.a.9.7 and reported iron screw stakes in position on a front of about 40 yards by 10 but that they had never been wired; just North of this the wire was strong but slack and only a few strands deep. 3 or 4 Germans were heard talking, no work appeared to be in progress. On the Left Sector our patrols reported nothing unusual.

INTELLIGENCE.
ENEMY WORK.
On our Right Sector during the night very little work appeared to be in progress. New wire and stakes about 8' long has been put up in front of the enemy's trenches from Q.5.d.9.15 to Q.6.c.11. Digging was in progress all day on the enemy's front and support line South of BEAUMONT HAMEL.

During the night our listening post in front of our wire at Q.10/11 could hear what seemed to be timber and iron being unloaded in BEAUMONT HAMEL.

Working parties were observed at Q.6.a.95 and in the trench running from Q.6.a.65.80 to Q.6.b.20.13.

ENEMY MOVEMENTS.
A party of 8 Germans were observed carrying sacks at Q.11.b.2.8. Two German Officers were observed at Q.5.d.8.3 - one looking at a map while the other was observing through glasses.

New stakes have been placed at Q.6.c.30.25. At 6.50 a.m. steam was observed rising from a trench at Q.6.a.20.100.

TRAIN MOVEMENTS.
The following train movements were observed:-
10.35 to ACHIET-LE-GRAND from BAPAUME.
11.20 to BAPAUME from ACHIET-LE-GRAND.

MISCELLANEOUS.
SEARCHLIGHT.
A Searchlight played on our lines between 10.45 p.m. and midnight and appeared to be in a motor car on the BEAUMONT ROAD.

FLARES.
At 9.30 p.m. two red flares were fired from the enemy's lines near BEAUMONT HAMEL. They were followed almost immediately by Artillery Fire.

BALLOONS.
At 7 a.m. a balloon was observed to rise from the wood BOIS de LOGEAST and descended at 3.10 p.m. At 7.35 a balloon rose near BUCQUOY at descended at 3.30 p.m. At 7.55 a balloon rose near LE-SARS and descended at 1 p.m.

21/5/16.

Captain, G.S.,
29th Division.

D.S.49.
22nd May, 16.

29th DIVISION DAILY SUMMARY.
For Period From
6.a.m. 21/5/16 to 6.a.m. 22/5/16.

OPERATIONS.

ARTILLERY.
Enemy artillery was unusually quiet in whole sector. One of our trenches in THIEPVAL WOOD was shelled at 12.45 a.m. and 3.p.m. with heavy H.E.
Our guns of various calibre registered during the day in the area of Q.5.c. and Q.4.d. at 9.p.m. heavy howitzers sent 4 shells into the enemy's line about Q.5.a.3.95. 3 seemed most effective.

TRENCH MORTARS.
Hostile Trench Mortars were rather active, firing into area Q.4.b.

PATROLS.
The SUNKEN Road Post was relieved at 9.p.m. During the relief and afterwards our machine guns on the Right and Left flank fired intermittently.
A listening patrol went out to Q.33. Considerable noise of hammering and singing was heard.
Another patrol of 1 Officer and 5 men reconnoitred in front from Q.14; no hostile patrols were encountered.

INTELLIGENCE.

ENEMY WORK.
At 4.p.m. 2 men were seen laying telephone cable coming from direction of BEAUCOURT. They got into a trench at point near Q.6.b.5.3. About 10 minutes later 3 men were observed following practically the same route.
Enemy is apparently busy all along his reserve line as small parties of men may be seen on the parapets nearly every hour of the day.
There were sounds of pile driving opposite Q.10.10.
Working parties are constantly seen at PENDANT COPSE
At 2.p.m. men were observed carrying sand bags at point Q.6.a.25.95.
Isolated cases of Germans seen carrying large sacks at Q.12.a.3.85. were observed.

ENEMY MOVEMENTS.
A considerable amount of transport was observed during the day coming from direction of GREVILLERS on road at point Q.22.d.67.
At @ 1.30.p.m. a party of about 30 men were seen coming from PYS.

TRAIN MOVEMENTS.
The following train movements were observed:-
7.25 to BAPAUME from LE - SARS.
9.20 to ACHIET - LE - GRAND from BAPAUME.

MISCELLANEOUS.

AEROPLANES - BALLOONS ETC.
3 Balloons were observed to rise at about 6.15 a.m.
A double bodied whitecoloured aeroplane flew over our lines at 8.50a.m. it was shelled by our A.A. Guns and returned at once to enemy area. Another hostile aeroplane was observed at about 10.20. It was also shelled and returned to enemy lines.

FLARES.
Very few flares were put up opposite our Sector which is rather unusual.

The Searchlight reported in yesterdays report was at magnetic bearing 115° North from Sap 5.
In enemy front line opposite Q.10.6 are 2 boards which are probably used as wind vanes. They are white, about 1' long and 8"wide and swing about in the wind.

Captain, G.S. 29th Div

29th DIVISION DAILY SUMMARY.
For Period From
3.a.m. 22/5/16 to 6.a.m. 23/5/16.

HEADQUARTERS
29th DIVISION
INTELLIGENCE
D.S. 50
23/5/16

OPERATIONS.

ARTILLERY.

Enemy Artillery at 9.a.m. fired several rounds all along the Right Sector (H.E. and Shrapnel).

Our Artillery was very quiet during the day.

At 10.30 p.m. the enemy commenced a bombardment of some intensity North of our Left Brigade Sector. The enemy seemed to be firing chiefly H.E. and Shrapnel. We replied to the bombardment with Shrapnel and H.E. Our Machine Guns in 2nd Avenue and WHITE CITY fired on the enemy's front line and wire. The enemy's Machine Guns were heard occasionally during the bombardment. Situation became normal again at 11.p.m.

A red light was sent up from the enemy's lines and remained visible for about 45 seconds. 5 minutes later a second red light was sent up. It was noticed that the enemy's fire diminished considerable. At 11.15 a green light was sent up but no action followed.

A few shells were put into MARY REDAN at 5.p.m.

PATROLS.

Officer patrolled wire round MARY REDAN. Nothing seen, also listened over mine by arrangement with Tunnelling Coy. to ascertained whether they could be heard on surface. Heard nothing.

The SUNKEN ROAD Post was withdrawn without difficulty at 11.20p.m. A Sniper in TENDERLOIN Street claims to have shot an enemy sniper on 22/5/16.

INTELLIGENCE.

ENEMY WORK.

In front of Q.10.b.47 enemy was digging and wiring during the night.

At 11.15 a.m. a working party was observed at point Q.6.a.96.

At daybreak men were seen in enemy SALIENT opposite Q.10.b 47. throwing water over parapet. When fired on operations ceased. In this salient much chalk appears to have been thrown up during the past few days. It is probable that the enemy is mining at this place. The whole salient is well under observation and is being carefully watched.

ENEMY MOVEMENTS.

Two men were seen behind BEAUMONT HAMEL at 3.30 p.m. they were dressed entirely in white and when fired on they doubled back to Communication trench.

TRAIN MOVEMENTS. The following train movements were observed:-
10.5. a.m. to BAPAUME from ACHIET - LE - GRAND.
1.30 p.m. to ACHIET - LE - GRAND from BAPAUME.

Trains were heard North from observation post Q.17.c.59. at 9.30. p.m and 10.15 p.m.

The train which is usually heard in BEAUMONT HAMEL between 8.30 and 8.45 p.m. was not heard last night until 10.45p.m.

MISCELLANEOUS.

PIGEONS.

2 pigeons were observed at 9.a.m. leaving the enemy's line and in the direction of MAILLY-MAILLET. At 5.30 a.m. 23/5/16 2 more pigeons were observed close to the enemy's lines flying North.

OBSERVATION POST.

An Observation Post exists at Q.5.d.7.5.

R. Lee
Captain G.S.
29th Division.

23rd May, 1916.

29th DIVISION DAILY SUMMARY.
For Period From
6.a.m. 23/5/16 to 6.a.m. 24/5/16.

> HEADQUARTERS.
> 29th DIVISION
> INTELLIGENCE.
> D.S.81.
> No. 24/5/16.
> Date....

OPERATIONS.

ARTILLERY.

The enemy fired 4 shrapnel shells at the BOWERY at 2.p.m. During the day the enemy sent about 12 H.E. shells on to the road near the SUCRERIE K.32.d. 15 rounds shrapnel (77 m.m.) was fire at the BROADWAY. No damage was done.

Enemy fired at interval throughout the day principally in the vicinity of New Work. FORT PROWSE was ranged on by the enemy, no damage was done.

Our Artillery was more active than usual during the day. Effective registering was observed at Q.5.a.3.1. to Q.5.a.3.5. At 7.p.m. some heavy shells were fired onto the enemy's line at Q.5.d.8.3. Our Artillery registered on the 'Y' Ravine in area Q.10.d.

PATROLS.

A patrol in charge of an Officer left our line at point Q.10.15.14 at 9.15 p.m. returning at Rooney's Sap at 10.30 p.m. The enemy were heard unloading iron and timber in BEAUMONT HAMEL. A mechanical excavator was heard working in the HAWTHORNE REDOUBT.

No enemy patrols were seen.

An Officer's patrol left our lines at 9.30 p.m. from Q.10.d.1.7. returning at 11.30 p.m., reports that enemy could be seen emptying sandbags in salient opposite, whilst a little further to the right a noise apparently made by a rope over a pulley could be heard.

INTELLIGENCE.

ENEMY WORK.

New wire and stakes were observed to have been placed at point Q.16.28.

AT 10.5. a.m. 2 men were observed to come from trench at point Q.5.b.70.58, each carrying cans, white bands on left arm, passed from view at point Q.5.b.68.60.

Sounds of wiring reported at Q.17.a.88.

Enemy was wiring and driving stakes at 12. p.m. opposite Q.16.6.

Steam has been observed at intervals issuing in puffs from a point about Q.10.d.78.95. near enemy front line. Some fresh earth has also been thrown up near this spot.

ENEMY MOVEMENTS.

Large enemy working party was seen during the afternoon in enemy trench which runs North and South in Q.6.a. & c.

At Q.6.c. 65.62 a party of about 30 were seen. Reported to Artillery who at 6.15.p.m fired at them, dispersing the party who, however, recommenced work about 30 minutes afterwards. At 7. p.m. 2 men were seen at a point about Q.5.d.40.50.. One was dressed in a long black coat and grey trousers and the other in grey coat and white trousers. They jumped into trench when fired on by our snipers (range 2000^x)%

One of our Snipers shot at a man in a front line trench near Q.10.d.85.35. The sniper apparently missed as immediately 3 caps appeared over the trench signalling "miss"

TRAINS At 12.p.m. a train was heard which stopped opposite MARY REDAN and afterwards sounds were heard like unloading rails and timber.

Trucks were heard running back from salient opposite Q.10.6. into BEAUMONT HAMEL.

24th May, 1916.

Ross Lee
Captain G.S.
29th Division.

29th DIVISION DAILY SUMMARY.
For Period From
6.a.m. 23/5/16 to 6.a.m 24/5/16.

HEADQUARTERS,
29th DIVISION,
INTELLIGENCE.

No. D.S.52.
Date 25/5/16.

OPERATIONS.

ARTILLERY.

Enemy artillery showed greater activity, particular attention being paid to the Support line and the Communication trenches at 1st Avenue, BROADWAY, BLOOMFIELD, and a new trench dug between 4th Avenue and KINGS Street.

5 rounds were fired into Southern part of AUCHONVILLERS shortly after 8.a.m. Shells were H.E. and very heavy.

About 10 rounds were fired at our lines from our right between 11.45 a.m. and 12.15 a.m. no casualties and not much damage done.

PATROLS.

A patrol under 2/Lieut Herbert, 16th Middlesex Regt, left at Q.4.10 to reconnoitre along front of wire and SUNKEN Road. No hostile patrols were met.

Officer's patrol left lines at 9.30 p.m. from Q.17.c.48. and returned at 1.a.m. at Q.17.a.51. Nothing to report.

INTELLIGENCE.

ENEMY MOVEMENTS.

Usual transport heard arriving at BEAUMONT HAMEL and sounds of pile driving in enemy's front line.

ENEMY WORK.

Enemy did not appear to be working so much as usual as things were very quiet opposite Q.16.b.1.9.

Many flares were also put up in this part of line.

Enemy appeared to be busy opposite Q.10.6. probably repairing damage done by our howitzers at 6.p.m.

Additional cover has been raised on supposed dug-outs at Q.5.a.31.

Stakes have been put up between front and second line at Q.4.d.85.15.

At 9.a.m. an enemy working party was observed at point Q.5.b.22. Another working party was also seen at point Q.6.a.86.

TRAIN ACTIVITY.

Train heard in BEAUMONT HAMEL at 3.50 p.m.
The following train movement was observed:-
12.30 to BAPAUME from ACHIET-LE-GRAND.

MISCELLANEOUS.

PIGEONS.

1 pigeon (supposed carrier) was seen to raise from Enemy's lines opposite Q.10.10 and fly in the direction of MAILLY-MAILLET.

SNIPERS.

2 enemy were shot at 7.a.m. opposite Q.16.5. and another opposite Q.10.5.2x at 6.15p.m.

There is a very low parapet at point Q.10.d.77.47.

Snipers in Left Sector claim to have wounded 2 of the enemy (a) 1 of a working party.
(b) hostile sniper.

W. M. Armstrong

25th May, 1916.

Captain G.S.
29th Division.

29th DIVISION DAILY SUMMARY.

For Period From
6.a.m. 26/5/16 to 6.a.m. 29/6/16

OPERATIONS.

ARTILLERY.

Enemy artillery showed great activity shelling BROADWAY, BLOOMFIELD, ESSEX STREET (with 77.mm. 6" guns traversed our front and support lines between LIMERICK JUNCTION and 2nd AVENUE, a few fell near 5th AVENUE and WHITE CITY. Slight damage was done to 2nd AVENUE.

At 9.30.a.m. they bombarded the Right Sector with H.E. and small shrapnel, but did no damage. At 3.30 p.m. a bombardment of section between Q.10.N.12 and Q.10.N.17 took place, the shells being 60.pdr. H.E. The old firing line was registered twice also D. and C. Streets. We had no casualties. About 40 shells were fired about 8 of which were blind.

Our Artillery retaliated on enemy front line and were registering during the day.

T.M. Gun in KING STREET ranged on the SUNKEN ROAD.

MACHINE GUNS

Enemy Machine Guns were inactive during the day except against our aeroplanes.

Machine gun firing at aeroplane was observed at point Q.17.b.20.21.

PATROLS.

Listening Posts at Q.10.8. Q.10.11 and Q.10.15. Posts at Q.10.8 and Q.10.11 report sounds as of a steam pump in use could be heard in enemy's lines opposite these points. Post at Q.10.15 reports all quiet.

Officer's patrol examined the ground along SUNKEN ROAD in Q.16.b. Nothing to report.

INTELLIGENCE

ENEMY MOVEMENTS

Between 11.a.m. and 1.p.m. about 100 horse wagons were seen travelling in both directions on BEAUCOURT ROAD.going towards
At 3.15 p.m. six men were observed working with truck on railway clearing in wood.

6.30 p.m. to transport wagons (horse) and about 50 men were seen on BEAUCOURT ROAD going towards BEAUCOURT.

At 4.45 p.m. three Germans were observed by F.O.O. opposite JACOB'S LADDER wearing grey uniforms. One had a dark hat with light band and one in a grey hat with white band, they were observing with glasses from their front line. Much horse transport could be observed passing to and from PYS on road at X.M1.d.68.

A party of about 40 men proceeding towards GREVILLERS on road at point G.22.d.67.

ENEMY WORK.

New chalk noticed in enemy line about Q.17.b.20.16.

Quantities of earth and chalk have been thrown up in enemy's second line at Y RAVINE.

Enemy wire hasv been strengthened at Q.10.b.75.85.

TRAIN ACTIVITY.

The following train movements were observed:-

9.45 to ACHIET-LE-GRAND from BAPAUME.
10.3 " " " " "
10.35 to BAPAUME from ACHIET-LE-GRAND.
10.55 " " " " "
11.45 " " from LESARS.
1.25 " ACHIET-LE-GRAND from BAPAUME.
4.p.m. " " " " "

TRAIN ACTIVITY (contd.)

4.20 p.m. to ACHIET-LE-GRAND from BAPAUME

MISCELLANEOUS

At 5.15 p.m. a carrier pigeon was seen to leave enemy's line and fly towards AUCHONVILLERS. Some flew over our lines at 6.50 p.m.

A unexploded 6" shell which came through the parapet at Q.10.12 was marked G.R.Z. 140
H.G. 15.

A considerable earth tremour was felt at 8.a.m. as if a mine had been exploded at a distance.

Much smoke was observed rising from trench at point Q.4.d.95, battery fired shots at said point.

W. M. Armstrong

26th May, 1916.

Captain, G.S.
29th Division.

29th DIVISION DAILY SUMMARY.

Period   From 6.a.m. 26/5/16 to 6.a.m. 27/5/16.

HEADQUARTERS.
29th DIVISION.
INTELLIGENCE.
No. DS 54
Date 27/5/16

OPERATIONS.

Artillery.   Enemy artillery was unusually active especially in early morning of 26th when many shells fell in the left sector.

Enemy artillery was also active shelling support and communication trenches with 6" shells, a few falling beyond dug-outs in WHITE CITY.

Considerable damage was done in ESSEX STREET and a dug-out in BLOOMFIELD was blown in.

Our artillery retaliated and volumes of smoke were seen to the left of BEAUMONT HAMEL and a good deal of damage was done to enemy trenches.

On our aeroplanes going up not a gun was heard (except A.A.) from enemy lines.

Machine Guns.   During the night enemy machine guns fired at irregular intervals both on firing line and supports.

Patrols.   A patrol under an N.C.O. went out at 10.15 p.m. and patrolled the ground on enemy's side of rise in front of our left sector, approximately Q.4.b.55. Everything was quiet.

Listening Posts at Q.10.8., Q.10.11 and Q.10.15. in front of our wire 30 yards out, occupied from 9.30.p.m to 2.0.a.m. All was quiet and no enemy patrols seen.

Snipers.   Two of the enemy were seen at sniping post Q.4.d.84, our guns dispersed them.

Sniper reports seing enemy sniper dressed in khaki.

Our snipers claim to have hit two of the enemy, in each case man was seen to fall.

INTELLIGENCE.

Enemy Work.   Between 11.a.m. and 12a.m. work noticed in progress about Q.17.b.20.16.   At 6.30.a.m. working party of about 50 men were seen near R.20.a.55.

Sounds of digging were reported in direction of SUNKEN ROAD, this was examined but no sap could be seen.

The wire in front of our line at Q.10.15.16 has been strengthened.

Fresh earth has been thrown up on enemy communication trench Q.11.a.87.

Enemy Movements.   Large bodies of troops were observed on road from PYS, M.1.b.73.

Enemy seen at point G.34 going in and out of wood.

In the right trench of salient opposite Q.10.1.7. noise as of an endless cable working was heard.

A number of enemy were noticed passing gaps in trench Q.10.d.25.60. about 6.0.p.m.

Six of enemy were seen on WAGGON ROAD at 2.5.p.m. dressed in very dark grey clothes with small round hats having what looked like a red band round them.

TRAIN ACTIVITY.   Two trains were observed from a point Q.10.6. running behind BEAUCOURT, one going South at 6.45.p.m and the other going North about 15 minutes later.

The following train movements were observed:

9.40. To ACHIET-LE-GRAND from BAPAUME.

-2-

Train Activity.(contd)
10.0. To ACHIET-LE-GRAND from BAPAUME.
10.10. To BAPAUME from ACHIET-LE-GRAND.
10.35. "   "   "   "   "
3.30. To ACHIET-LE-GRAND from BAPAUME.
4.0. "   "   "   "   "
4.30. To ACHIET-LE-GRAND from BAPAUME.
5.45. To BAPAUME TO ACHIET-LE-GRAND.

MISCELLANEOUS.

        Fuses of shell picked up in B.Street yesterday was marked as follows:- G.r.Z.140.
                      E x G 15.
and was passed on to artillery.

        A nose cap of an A.A. shell made of aluminium was picked up marked   Dopp 2 96
                                       Sp.
time fuse was set for 43".

        A light was observed last night somewhere on the MAILLY-SUCERIE ROAD, it was bright at first and faded away. Just after this light appeared trench mortars and artillery opened up on the REDAN.

        At Q.11.b.25.26. there is what appears to be an iron door or shutter and near it a cut in the bank which might be an emplacement. Behind iron door there is ~~a small~~ structure like a dug-out.

        Three hostile balloons were over LE-SARS, BUCQUOY, BOIS-DE-LOGEAST.

27th May 1916.   Captain G.S.
                                                                  29th Division.

29th DIVISION DAILY SUMMARY.
For Period From
6.a.m. 27/5/16 to 6.a.m. 28/5/16.

> HEADQUARTERS.
> 29th DIVISION.
> INTELLIGENCE.
> No. 55 55
> Date 28/5/16

OPERATIONS

ARTILLERY.
Enemy's artillery was fairly quiet. 2 H.E. shells fell in our support line near LIMERICK JUNCTION. 7 shrapnel shells on Sap 8 but they appeared to be firing at Sap 7. AUCHONVILLERS came in for some shelling and also the new trench from FOURTH AVENUE to KING STREET. A dug-out was blown in in St.PATRICK'S AVENUE.
D.STREET and FIRST AVENUE were shelled with 9,H.E. between 4.15.p.m. and 5.p.m. 4 of these were "Blind".

MACHINE GUNS.
Enemy's guns at Q.10.d.67. and Q.10.d.79. and Q.16.d.70.80. were active against our aeroplanes.

PATROLS
Listening Posts at Q.10.8. Q.10.11 and Q.10.15 in front of our wire about 30 yards out were posted at 9.30.a.m. and withdrawn at 2.a.m. They reported enemy digging in Y RAVINE, usual train and transport heard arriving at BEAUMONT HAMEL. No Enemy Patrols seen.
An enemy party of about 8 was seen leaving Enemy Trenches in Salient Q.10.d. at dusk last evening. They were also seen to return this morning. They were probably a listening patrol or covering party.

SNIPERS.
Our Snipers shot a man who exposed himself near Q.10.d.77.47. This man was probably an artillery observer as he was using field glasses and enemy artillery was firing on our trenches at the time.
Two of our snipers were posted at daybreak at a point in hedge near SUNKEN ROAD Q.16.b. about a 100 yards in front of our line. They returned safely at dusk. Nothing to report.

INTELLIGENCE.

ENEMY WORK.
Q4 d 4/3
Working parties were heard North and South of SUNKEN ROAD. they were dispersed by M.G.Fire.
Work was continued on enemy's line immediately in front of BEAUMONT. Quantities of earth and chalk have been thrown up in second line at Y RAVINE.
On the South side of Y RAVINE a new trench has been dug which straightens out a small re-entrant at point approximately Q.10.d.55.75.
Work was reported in progress near Q.17.b.20.16. and sounds were heard resembling pile driving.
At 11.p.m. wiring was heard opposite point MARY REDAN. The party were fired on among us.
Enemy working party was observed in his front line during the whole day, carrying brushwood and planks, also occasionally shovelling up earth.
Working parties were observed in trench at points Q.6.a.25.90 and Q.6.b.22.

ENEMY MOVEMENTS.
Much horse transport and small parties of men were observed passing to and from PYS at M.1.d.49.
Wagon traffic as usual.
Train activity. A train was heard at 9.15.p.m. apparently entering BEAUMONT HAMEL from BEAUSSART.
The following train movements were observed:-
8.15 to ACHIET-LE-GRAND from BAPAUME
9.55 " " " " "
10.12 " " " " "
10.40 " BAPAUME from ACHIET-LE-GRAND.

TRAIN ACTIVITY (Contd.)
10.53 to BAPAUME from ACHIET-LE-GRAND.
11.2. "   "   "   "   "   "
12.0. "   "   "   LE-SARS.
12.24. " ACHIET-LE-GRAND from BAPAUME.

MISCELLANEOUS.
(a) A Searchlight was observed at 9.20 p.m. Northwest of our line.
(b) Enemy sent up a Red flare near BEAUMONT HAMEL at 10.p.m.
(c) Our Sniper claims to have hit an enemy Officer observing in the front line.
(d) A well has been spotted in BEAUMONT HAMEL (Map ref. later.) where fresh chalk has been thrown up, work continues here and it is suggested that the old well is now a main shaft.
(e) Smoke or stem was observed at 3.45.a.m. this morning coming in distinct puffs from a point about Q.10.d.65.80 in trench in enemy salient. This has been noticed before on several occasions. A little later a considerable quantity of smoke was seen coming from point marked 7747 in Q.10.d.

W. M. Armstrong
Captain G.S.
29th Division.

28th May, 1916.

29th DIVISION DAILY SUMMARY.
For Period From 6.a.m. 28/5/16 to 6.a.m. 29/5/16

> HEADQUARTERS.
> 29th DIVISION.
> INTELLIGENCE.
> 29/5/16

OPERATIONS.

ARTILLERY.
Enemy registered on St.HELENS Trench about 4.p.m. placing 1 shell in the trench. Several shells fell near WHITE CITY, 30. to 40 yards West of Battalion Headquarters, possibly overs, several fell much nearer front line.

MACHINE GUNS.
Machine Gun from Q.17.b.20.21 was active at intervals against our aeroplanes.

PATROLS. (listening post)
A small standing patrol which left Q.10.7. at 9.30 p.m. reports the sound of rails and wood being dumped, in an N.N.E. direction, which they cannot specify more accurately; also what sounded like a motor on a light railway, the sound of which came from the direction of BEAUMONT HAMEL.

INTELLIGENCE.

ENEMY WORK.
Considerable activity continued to be shewn at the point Q.10.d.55.70. At 8.30. p.m. sound of wiring was heard. From 5. p.m. to 1.p.m. sounds of spade work. The position is being closely watched.

A considerable of amount work has been done recently to the enemy front line about Q.17.a.95.50., as a heap of chalk there is steadly increasing. During the night iron was heard being moved about.

Usual engine activity heard in enemy salient Q.10.d.

At 3.30.a.m. e explosions took place in enemy trenches left of BEAUMONT HAMEL in front of Q.10.15 (bay 24.) which suggested fairly extensive operations (blasting). At each explosion smoke rose in a bluish white cloud. Digging is also reported near this point.

More stakes and wire have been placed at point Q.5.a.8.3.

A working party was observed at point Q.6.a.9.5.

ENEMY MOVEMENTS.
4 Germans were seen working just behind front line trench in salient Q.10.d., wearing grey uniform with round hat around which was a white or light blue band.

2 Germans were observed at 8.35 p.m. in a shell crater 150 yards from our wire near HAWTHORNE REDOUBT. They were fired on by us with Lewis Gun by the light of a Very Light result not known.

At 3.35 a party of troops of about 50 were observed coming from the direction of GREVILLERS on the road at point G.22.d.6.7.

TRAINS AND TRANSPORT.
Enemy transport entering BEAUMONT HAMEL was normal during the night except for the period between 11.15 p.m. and 11.25. p.m, when the volume of sound was louder. The following train movements were observed:-
10.   to ACHIET-LE-GRAND from BAPAUME.
10.15."   "   "   "   "
10.45 "   "   "   "   "
10.50 "   BAPAUME   "   ACHIET-LE-GRAND.
11.   "   "   "   "   "
12.20 "   ACHIET-LE-GRAND   "   BAPAUME.

MISCELLANEOUS. The notice board put out by the enemy has been moved during the night 27/28th inst. It is in good view in front of their wire

29th May, 1916.   Captain G.S.
                                                   29th Division.

29th DIVISIONAL SUMMARY.
For Period From
6.a.m. 29/5/16 to 6.a.m. 30/5/16

HEADQUARTERS.
29th DIVISION.
INTELLIGENCE.
No. D.S.57
Date. 30/5/16

OPERATIONS.

ARTILLERY.

Enemy artillery fired about 30 shells into ACHEUX on the morning of the 29th. Little damage however was done. It is thought that these guns are in BEAUREGARD WOOD, L.28.c. 60.30.

About 15 shrapnel shells fell about 9.a.m. just West of White City near 5th Avenue. Several shells also fell between WHITE CITY and firing line to our left at the same time In the afternoon the road going North from AUCHONVILLERS was shelled. 6 "blinds" in succession were observed.

Our own Artillery opened fire at 9.30.p.m. and again at 10.15.p.m. on the SUNKEN ROAD Q.4.d.4.4. An enemy working party had been heard at this spot at 9.30 and was not heard afterwards.

MACHINE GUNS.

Enemy Machine guns were chiefly active against our air craft.

SNIPERS.

At 8.15. a.m. a German sniper was located lying in front of salient opposite Q.10.6. A sergt. crawled out on the ground overlooking ESSEX Street and was firedon by enemy sniper. He returned the fire and reported a positive hit. Body of enemy lay there until 11.p.m. when 2 Germans crawled from enemy trench showing white flag with red cross on and carried the body back. When the party reached enemy parapet flag was lowered and we again fired on them. They descended hurridly into trench.

At 9.a.m. a German observed walking on top of trenches in HAWTHORNE REDOUBT, carrying 2 cans. Our sniper fired on the man who dropped cans and limped a short distance before he jumped into trench.

INTELLIGENCE.

ENEMY WORK.

(1) A wiring party in fron of Q.10.d.55.70 was dispers with Lewis Gun fire at 1.a.m.

(2) The usual sounds of digging at the point of the salient Q.10.d.55.70 were heard, and puffs as from an engine at about 11.p.m. and again at 4.a.m. apparently from quarry at Q.11.d.52.17.

(3) About 10.p.m. the sounds of supposed enemy mining were heard from a deep dug-out from the junction of FETHARD Stree and 'G' Street. At 11.50. p.m. work was stopped in the vicinity a a listener was posted in the dug-out all night, with the result that sounds of tapping, picking and driving of timber were heard 4 times between 11.30.p.m. and 12.40.a.m.

(4) An enemy engine is again reported in 'Y' RAVINE. Enemy working party were noticed at intervals during the day in BEAUMONT HAMEL. Artillery fire a few rounds and parties ceased wo

ENEMY MOVEMENTS.

Several men were observed going along the road in BEAUMONT HAMEL about 3.p.m.. 1 man appeared to be in civilian clothes about 7.25.

TRAINS AND TRANSPORT.

The amount of transport heard was about the normal and was only audible during the earlier part of the night.

6 horse transport wagons were observed coming from PYS, passed from view at point M.1.b. 6.3.

5 horse transport wagons and 1 motor transport were observed going towards PYS on road at point M.1.d.4.9.

At 4.35. 2 horse transport wagons and 2 horsemen going

in the direction of GREVILLERS on road on point G.22.d.6.7.
The following train movements were observed.
9.25 to ACHIET-LE-GRAND from BAPAUME.
10.15 to BAPAUME from ACHIET-LE-GRAND.
10.53 "   "   "   "   "   "
 3.50. " ACHIET-LE-GRAND from BAPAUME.
 5.50 "   "   "   "   "   "

MISCELLANEOUS.

(a) A German dressed in a bluish green uniform was seen at about 6.p.m. at about Q.11.c.90.75.

(b) During the afternoon the enemy appeared to be using sprayer on the parapet of the front trench from Q.10.d.55.70 to Q.10d/60.80, though with what object is not known

By means of a glass stuck in the parados of a German trench in HAWTHORNE REDOUBT, we were able to see Germans sitting in trench and reading newspapers. One was noticed wearing a F.S. cap with a white band on.

(c) NOTICE BOARD.

The notice board put up by the Germans on 20th inst. at Q.4.d.6.5. has been moved forward. It bore the following inscription. Lieut Uren is dead and burried what about Vishof Lehman.
We have put out a board with the following reply:-
KARL LEHMANN ist gestorben ein kreuzmit seinem namen steht anf seinen grab.

(d) Well.   The well in BEAUMONT HAMEL is

at Q 5 c 6.3.

W. M. Armstrong
                                          Captain G.S.
30th May, 1916.   29th Division.

Appendix 15

HEADQUARTERS.
29th DIVISION.
INTELLIGENCE.
No. AS 58
Date 31/7/16

29th DIVISION DAILY SUMMARY for
Period   From 6.a.am 30/5/16 to 6.a.m. 31/5/16.

OPERATIONS.

Artillery.   Q.10.4. and the Sector between Q.16.b.3.8. and Q.17.a.10.35. came in for some shelling in the morning. Our aeroplanes also were fired on with shrapnel and machine guns. Our artillery retaliated at 6.30.p.m. by bombarding the enemy's front line from about Q.10.d.6.6. to Q.10.d.9.3. About 9.a.am. the junction of GABION AVENUE and WHITHINGTON AVENUE was shelled with shrapnel; during the morning some H.E. fell close to the junction of LIGHT RAILWAY and Road in Q.14.b. Soon after 10.30.a.m. a few shells passed over the MOULIN REDOUBT without doing any damage. ST.HELEN'S was shelled with "whizz bangs" from 6.0. to 7.30.a.m. - no damage done.   A Minenwerfer fell just behind our front line apparently aimed at MINDEN TERRACE.

Our own artillery shelled the SUNKEN ROAD at 11.p.m. Q 4 & 4/4.

Machine Guns.   Enemy machine gun activity was normal - chiefly against our aircraft.

Patrols.   At 11.p.m. 1 Officer and 5 Other Ranks left Sap at Q.17.19. and discovered an enemy wiring party working along with covering party close to our wire. Lewis guns were at once turned on them.

At midnight a patrol consisting of 2 Officers and 6 Other Ranks left No.2 Sap (South of Mary Redan) and investigated wire up to a point of the REDAN thereafter going due East for about 140 yards to within 30 yards of enemy wire. The ground there is level except where broken by shelling. Nothing suspicious was heard.

At 10.30.p.m. an Officers' patrol examined the Road Q.10.3. and the dead ground adjacent, and found nothing of moment to report.

Snipers.   A sniper was located at Q.17.a.85.80. Machine Gun fire was directed on to that point and the sniping ceased.

INTELLIGENCE.

Enemy Movements.   About 3.30.p.m. three successive pairs of the enemy were seen leaving a trench and moving along WAGON ROAD in northerly direction dressed in Dark Blue Uniforms.

Normal movements were seen in BEAUMONT HAMEL.

Two heavy guns were seen firing from BEAUREGARD, point L.2.c.5015. One seems to be between first and second gaps in trees, the other slightly to the right of second gap in trees.

Enemy Work.   Listening Posts at Q.10.8. and Q.10.11. reported enemy busy putting up wire to their front.

At 6.30.p.m. white chalk was observed to be thrown up from about Q.11.c.6.5.

Trains and Transport.   Six motor transport wagons were observed coming from the direction of GREVILLERS on road at point G.22.d.67.

Between 9.30.p.m. and 10.10.p.m. transport was heard moving very slowly in the direction of BEAUMONT HAMEL. Our artillery fired four shells in the direction and the pace at once accelerated. The noise continued till 12.30.a.m

-2-

12.30.a.m. Sounds like the dumping of iron rails were also audible.

The following train movements were observed:-

7.15 To BAPAUME from LE SARS.
9.20 TO ACHIET-LE-GRAND from BAPAUME.
3.30 "   "   "   "   "   "
3.52 "   "   "   "   "   "
5.0   "   "   "   "   "   "

v MISCELLANEOUS.

Projectiles. Four nose-caps were picked up in the neighbourhood of FORT PROWSE. The numbers and marks on them are as follows:-

Dopp.Sb Z^C/ 91.   Gr. Z. 14o
                                471 MA 15.

K.Z. 14° K.Z. 14.
N.S.U. 15.   A.W. 15.
  183

Suspected Mining. Listeners were stationed throughout the night in the dug-out at junction of C.STREET and PETHARD STREET, but no suspicious sounds were heard.

W.M. Armstrong.

                                             Captain, G.S.
31st May 1916.   29th Division.

www.ingramcontent.com/pod-product-compliance
Lightning Source LLC
Chambersburg PA
CBHW081356160426

43192CB00013B/2418